TAXPAYERS DON'T STAND A CHANCE

WHY BATTLEGROUND OHIO LOSES NO MATTER WHO WINS
(AND WHAT TO DO ABOUT IT)

MATT A. MAYER

TWITTER: @OHIOMATT

FACEBOOK:

WWW.FACEBOOK.COM/TAXPAYERSDONTSTANDACHANCE

WWW.OPPORTUNITYOHIO.ORG

PROVISUM STRATEGIES LLC

Other Books by Matt A. Mayer

HOMELAND SECURITY AND FEDERALISM: PROTECTING AMERICA FROM OUTSIDE THE BELTWAY (*WITH FOREWARD BY THE HONORABLE EDWIN MEESE III*)

Provisum Strategies LLC
P.O. Box 98
Dublin, Ohio 43017-0098

First Provisum Strategies LLC edition July 2012

For information about special discounts for bulk purchases, please contact Provisum Strategies at
checkmate@provisumstrategies.com.

Cover Designed by John Fleming

Manufactured in the United States of America

Library of Congress Cataloguing-in-Publication Data is available.

ISBN-13: 978-1469985091

ISBN-10: 1469985098

This book is dedicated to the millions of men, women, and children who rose up as part of the Tea Party and 9-12 movements in defense of America's and Ohio's futures. Though often disparaged by the media and paid only lip service to by most politicians, they represent the greatest tradition in American history—telling our political leaders, "Enough!"

This book is also dedicated to those people who helped me along the way. To Sam Duff who hired me for two summers at his landscape company where I learned the value of hard, physical work. To Rick O'Donnell who freed me from the monotonous life of a lawyer and allowed me to excel in the world of politics and policy. To Walt Klein whose wise counsel and father-like mentorship helped me navigate through sometimes treacherous waters. To Jim Carafano for giving me the opportunity to be part of the world's top think tank and contribute to our national dialogue on how best to secure America. To the folks in the State Policy Network for providing me guidance and support that proved critical in rescuing the Buckeye Institute from financial ruin and policy irrelevance.

And, finally, to my wife, Jessica, and three kids, Madeleine, Genevieve, and Sebastian, for providing much-needed support, for serving as constant reminders about what it is we are fighting to preserve, and for injecting a little balance when I needed it most.

CONTENTS

TAXPAYERS DON'T STAND A CHANCE

100 PERCENT OF NET PROCEEDS FROM THE SALE OF THIS BOOK WILL BE DONATED TO THE RONALD REAGAN PRESIDENTIAL FOUNDATION & LIBRARY AND THINK TANK MEMBERS IN THE STATE POLICY NETWORK.

PREFACE

This book is not about the federal government and Washington, D.C. So much of our thoughts and actions focus on what happens federally that we ignore far more important and impactful events in our own backyard. Parts of this book will discuss federal issues, but with Ohio serving as a perpetual battleground state nationally, I wanted to focus on what's been happening in Ohio over the last two decades.

Based on an exhaustive review of the data, travels around the state, and first-hand experience with our political leaders, I came to the conclusion that without fundamental reforms taxpayers in Ohio don't stand a chance of escaping higher taxes and a systemically weak economy, especially compared to other states. Equally disappointing, this conclusion remains valid regardless of which political party wins, as neither party has the courage, skill, or commitment to truly fix Ohio.

Why is what I have to say about Ohio worth listening to? After all, I am not an "expert" sitting high in an ivory tower of academia pondering things big and small. I am not a long-serving elected official with years of experience to share. I am not a famous talking head who appears on television regularly. Frankly, I am an Ohioan just like you.

Beyond my love for this state, I have several qualifications that provide me with unique and worthwhile insights—namely my heritage, my middle-class upbringing, and my career path.

I am a sixth generation Daytonian. My ancestors immigrated from Germany, arriving in Dayton in the 1830s. They were farmers and tradesmen who hoped for a better life in America.

My entrepreneurial great-grandfather started the Joseph A. Kroger Groceries & Hardware store in Dayton in 1906. Unfortunately, it wasn't THAT Kroger grocery store. He and his family lived above the store for a period of time. My grandpa was born in 1911. In 1920, with eleven kids, Joseph started the Standard Seed & Premium Spice Company, which my grandpa and his brother took over and ran until 1973 when my grandpa retired at the age of sixty-two.

None of these ancestors had more than a high school education.

My mom was born in 1944. She didn't graduate from college either. My dad graduated from the University of Dayton with a physical education degree. He served in Vietnam and then became a gym teacher at Colonel White High School in Dayton. He left teaching shortly after I was born because the pay wasn't enough to make ends meet with four kids.

For most of my childhood, my mom was a stay-at-home mom. In 1985, she got a part-time, entry-level job as a customer service representative at a call center working nights. Eventually, my mom became a manager. After 26 years with the company, she retired at the age of sixty-eight. My dad mostly worked in the electronics industry, but spent his last working years in low-level service jobs. He stopped working in 2008 at the age of 64.

I was born in Dayton in 1971, but grew up mostly in Westerville, Ohio. I started working at the age of 12 as a newspaper carrier for the now-defunct *Columbus Citizen-Journal* and then *The Columbus Dispatch*. By the time I graduated from college, I had worked as a grocery store bag boy, a pizza maker, an ice cream cone maker, a hotel maid, a college resident assistant, a landscaper, and a restaurant server.

I have five brothers and sisters (an accountant, a nurse, an IT technician, a elementary school teacher, and an architect project manager). We all went to college, with five of us earning bachelor degrees and one earning an associate degree. Except for my older sister, all of my siblings have lived their entire adult lives in Ohio. I am the only one who went to graduate school. I am married, and we live in Dublin, Ohio, with our three kids.

As this brief family account details, my heritage as an Ohioan spans occupations from immigrant farmers to public servants to professionals and typifies the American Dream and the gradual educational rise across generations. I experienced first-hand the urban decay in Dayton as my grandparents' neighborhood went from one where we as kids could walk down to the local drugstore for candy to one where their garage was routinely tagged by vandals.

I also experienced first-hand the growth of Columbus' suburbs. Dublin went from one high school to three. Westerville exploded. Powell, Olentangy, Gahanna, and Hilliard boomed. The places I went as a kid in Westerville largely closed down: Brownie's Market, Bob Kenney's barbershop, the Super Duper grocery store, the Elder Beerman's shoe store, State Savings Bank, the Little Professor bookstore, Gold Circle Mall, Cockerell's restaurant, and Friendly's restaurant. Thankfully, Schneider's Bakery, Yogi Hoagies, and the Dairy Queen remain. A few got bigger: the Donatos Pizza and the Westerville Public Library expanded a bit and St. Paul's Church doubled the number of classrooms and just built a new mega-church.

At the same time, as recently highlighted by the *Dispatch*, the north Columbus area where I went to high school at St. Francis DeSales has changed. Northland Mall—decimated by the arrivals of Polaris Fashion Place and Easton Town Center—has been torn down and replaced with government buildings. Many of the Italian families have moved north and have been replaced by immigrant Hispanic and Somali families.

While I didn't experience the devastation up in Cleveland, Toledo, or Youngstown, my family's middle class existence provided me with lots of experiences and instilled in me many valuable lessons.

Equally important, I am one of the few Ohioans who left and came back.

After one year of practicing law in Columbus, I headed West like so many Ohioans. I moved to Colorado and its 300 plus days of sunshine per year. I practiced law for a few years where my last legal work involved representing the Secretary of State in Colorado's redistricting legal battle. Shortly thereafter, I took a 50 percent pay-cut to run a congressional campaign for a first time candidate. Outspent by a five-to-one ratio and outmanned in paid staff by a ten-to-one ratio, we lost the primary to the eventual general election winner (and Colorado Republican Party Chairman and owner of a $300 million bank) by roughly 1,900 votes, which earned both my candidate and me "Rising Star" awards.

I then became the Deputy Director of the Colorado Department of

Regulatory Agencies under Governor Bill Owens in 2003. We instituted an aggressive regulatory reform effort to help free Colorado businesses from the burden of unnecessary regulations. As part of that reform, our top-notch IT staff created an award-winning online tool citizens could use to track new and amended regulations. That system served as a model for the system put in place in Ohio in 2009 (Ohio is always a laggard).

When I received the call from the Bush Administration to join the newly formed U.S. Department of Homeland Security, we packed up and headed to Washington, D.C., despite the fact that a loss in November 2004 by George W. Bush would have meant the unemployment line for me. The opportunity to help secure America from the terrorist threat of Islamic jihadists was one I simply couldn't pass up.

Our time in Washington proved highly educational, but deeply frustrating. We found that the place really is consumed with accumulating power and that many people there rarely have the taxpayers' best interest in mind when they act. States and their constitutional role are mere afterthoughts. I saw colleagues abuse their positions to skip airport security lines so they didn't have to wait like the rest of us had to. I watched bureaucrats undermine reforms by slow-rolling directives. I noticed government contractors embed themselves into the system and expand their roles aggressively. I observed incompetent people rise, good people fall, and a total lack of meaningful accountability.

Three years in that swamp was enough for us. Because we wanted our two kids to be closer to family, we decided to focus our job search on Ohio. With the horrendous Ohio election results in November 2006,

I thought that the conservative movement could use all the help it could get in getting Ohio back on track. So, we returned to Ohio.

My experiences in Colorado, Virginia, and Washington, D.C., provide me with ideas that could be used to reform Ohio.

Next, though I am a Republican, I am and always have been first and foremost a conservative. Unlike many of my brethren, I am not an apologist or Kool-aid drinker for Republican politicians. I believe the best way to help politicians is to be as honest and objective as possible with them. Those politicians who surround themselves with straphangers tend to perform poorly, as they lack someone who can provide desperately needed contrarian advice. I also have found that the most successful politicians demand candid advice and disdain yes men. I always have done my best to call a spade a spade regardless of party affiliation and will criticize my side as much as the other side when they make bad decisions.

Finally, over the last couple of years, I ran the Buckeye Institute for Public Policy Solutions, a free market think tank focused on economic freedom and competitiveness, entrepreneurship and job creation, and government transparency and accountability. I spent more than 7,000 hours reviewing and analyzing economic data, testifying on key reforms, meeting with political leaders, talking with media outlets, debating the issues, and developing solutions to Ohio's toughest challenges.

In two and a half years, I traveled over 16,000 miles (16,301 to be precise) criss-crossing the state and speaking to more than 15,000 Ohioans. I had the privilege of seeing vast stretches of Ohio—big cities, small villages, colleges, K-12 schools, businesses, farms, and many fields, of course. I had the even greater privilege of meeting so many patriotic men, women, and children who care so deeply about our state and country. These Ohioans came from all sides of the political spectrum and from all walks of life.

My time at the Buckeye Institute allowed me to develop a deeper, data-driven understanding of Ohio and the problems it faces. As chapter one discusses, those problems are big and the solutions offered over the last two decades have done little to solve those problems.

With these "qualifications" in mind, I hope you find this book insightful and worth the time you put into reading it. If you don't like what I propose to again make Ohio the great state it once was, what are your solutions beyond maintaining the status quo?

*   *   *

Two quick notes on the book. Throughout the book I use the city of Dublin, its school district, and one of its townships to illustrate points. I use Dublin entities for two reasons: first, as a resident, I am most familiar with it and, secondly, I think it is important to shine a light on entities within my sphere rather than ignore what is in my own backyard in favor of places where I can highlight problems from a distance without worrying how my comments will impact me, my family, and my community. The fact is that the issues I highlight are occurring in jurisdictions across Ohio and America.

From time to time I insert a "JINO Alert." As you'll come to read, a JINO is a Journalist in Name Only, and it refers to those journalists who allow their liberal bias to impact how they cover Ohio. The JINO Alert contains suggestions for JINOs and for citizen investigative reporters on items they could cover to provide critical information to voters.

1

OHIO'S FALL FROM POWER

Horace Greeley: "Go West [and South], young man [and woman]!"

The Land of Presidents

From statehood in 1803 to 1923, Ohio was either the birthplace or home of eight presidents. William Henry Harrison, the ninth and shortest-serving president, lived in Hamilton County, Ohio, when he was elected in 1840. Following the 1868 election, Ulysses S. Grant, born in Point Pleasant, Ohio, became the 18th president and served two full terms. Rutherford B. Hayes, born in Delaware, Ohio, followed Grant and served as the 19th president despite losing the popular vote in the 1876 election. James Garfield, born in Moreland Hills, Ohio, followed Hayes as the 20th president in 1881, but, like Harrison, only served a short time before being assassinated. Benjamin Harrison, grandson of William Henry Harrison, was born in North Bend, Ohio, and became the 23rd president. William McKinley, born in Miles, Ohio, served as the 25th president after winning both the 1896 and 1900 elections, but was assassinated in 1901. After the 1908 election, William Howard Taft, born in Cincinnati, became the 27th president.

Wadsworth 9.12
Liberty Scholarship
Pledge Card

I am willing to contribute to the Wadsworth 9.12 Liberty
Scholarship fund to benefit worthy local graduating seniors from
high school or home school, and/ or students already enrolled in
higher education.

I am able to donate the amount of _____ by May 31, 2013.

_____

Signature

_____

Printed name

_____

Email address

_____

Phone number

- -

Please make checks payable to: Wadsworth 912 Group
And reference "scholarship" on the memo line of your check.

Donations may be mailed to: Wadsworth 912 Group
P.O Box 986
Wadsworth, OH 44282

"Although the Wadsworth 9.12 Group is a non-profit corporation,
donations are not considered to be tax deductible."

Finally, in 1920, Warren G. Harding, born in Blooming Grove, Ohio, became the 29th president, but died in office in 1923.

From 1804 to 1923, a period of 119 years, Ohio was the birthplace or home of eight presidents out of 27, or 30 percent. From 1923 through at least 2016, a period of 93 years, Ohio has not been the birthplace or home of any of the 15 presidents (and possibly 16 if Governor Mitt Romney wins in 2012). The closest Ohio has come to having another president rested in Charles Dawes, who served as President Calvin Coolidge's vice president from 1925 to 1929.

The two most recent runs for the presidency by Ohioans involve the failed five-month presidential run of now-Governor John Kasich in 1999 and Congressman Dennis Kucinich's Hail Mary runs in 2004 and 2008. Many pundits believe Senator Rob Portman is Ohio's best hope of producing a president. In contrast, since President Harding, more than half—eight out of 15—of the presidents have come from the South or West of the United States, with seven out of the last nine (1963 to 2009) coming from Texas, California, Arkansas, and Georgia.

The Land of Economic Power

Economically, a decade before my grandfather was born in 1911, Ohio's per capita income was 9.7 percent above the national average. When my mom was born in 1944, Ohio's per capita income was 10 percent above the national average. When I was born in 1971, Ohio's per capita income had fallen to 0.4 percent below the national average. And when my son was born in Columbus in 2010, Ohio's per capita income had dropped to 9.4 percent below the national average. In roughly 100 years and four generations, Ohio went from an economic leader in America to an economic laggard.

On the jobs front, Ohio's economy is among the weakest in America. From January of 1990 to April 2012, Ohio netted just 245,600 private sector jobs, which is a paltry 6 percent increase over the course of 22 years. During the booming 1990s, Ohio added 713,600 private sector jobs, but that growth only ranked as the 38th best in the United States. In the lost decade of the 2000s, Ohio bled more jobs—614,100 jobs—than every state except Michigan, leaving it with the second worst job market in America. Ohio's job growth ranking from 1990 to today is the 5th worst, behind only New Jersey, Michigan, Rhode Island, and Connecticut.

Of the ten private sector industries tracked by the U.S. Bureau of Labor Statistics, four have fewer jobs today in Ohio than in January 1990 (Mining & Logging; Construction; Manufacturing; and Information). Four other industries have fewer jobs today than in January 2000 (Trade, Transportation & Utilities; Financial Activities; Leisure & Hospitality; and Other Services). Only two industries— Professional & Business Services and government run or government-funded Education & Health Services—have more jobs today than in either January 1990 or January 2000.

Since 2000, Ohio's private sector has lost 10 percent of its jobs. Without adjusting for population growth, it likely will take until November 2018 for Ohio's private sector to return to the number of jobs possessed in March 2000 (4.85 million). If that prediction comes to pass, a child born in the peak month (March 2000) would be in her first semester of college when Ohio regains its lost jobs.

To put these figures in perspective, the number of government workers in Ohio grew by 51,900 from January 1990 to April 2012, or a full 21 percent of the net private sector job growth. Despite the global economic crisis, from January 2000 to April 2012, the number of government workers in Ohio has only declined by 12,300 jobs, a 1.6 percent decline.

For those keeping score on job losses, it is -468,000 in the private sector (-9.7 percent) versus -12,300 in government (-1.6 percent).

An even starker picture comes in to view when you look at Ohio's job market as a percentage of population. In 1990, Ohio possessed 10,847,115 people and 4,126,800 private sector jobs, which meant that 38.9 percent of Ohioans worked in the private sector. As of 2000, Ohio stood at 11,353,140 people and 4,841,200 private sector jobs, so 42.6 percent of Ohioans worked in the private sector. By 2010, Ohio had grown to 11,536,504 people, but saw its private sector shrink to 4,226,900 jobs. As a result, as a percentage of population, only 36.6 percent of Ohioans now work in the private sector, a 2.3 percent reduction from 1990. So, even though the total number of jobs from 1990 to 2010 increased, after adjusting for population, this far more accurate number shows just how bad things really have been in Ohio.

A similar look at government jobs also reveals a problem. In 1990, Ohio employed 713,600 government workers, which equated to 15 percent of non-farm jobs. By 2000, there were 779,100 government workers in Ohio, comprising 14 percent of non-farm jobs. Even though Ohio added 65,500 government jobs, because of private sector job growth those jobs represented a slightly smaller share of non-farm jobs. By 2010, however, despite the loss of 614,100 private sector jobs, Ohio employed even more government workers: 782,100, which captured 16 percent of the non-farm jobs.

When the explosion in the heavily government funded Education & Health Services industry is added to this analysis, the picture becomes even more imbalanced. In 1990, those two industries employed 1,249,300 Ohioans, with the remaining non-farm industries employing 3,592,500 people. That means that a full 26 percent of jobs came from government-dependent industries. By 2000, the figures were 1,451,400 and 4,168,300, respectively, with government-dependent industries still employing 26 percent of Ohioans. By 2010, dramatic changes had occurred as the decade saw large gains in the Education & Health Services industry and huge losses in the Manufacturing; Construction; Trade, Transportation, & Utilities; and Information industries. The two government-dependent industries employed 1,618,100 Ohioans versus 3,390,400 in the other non-farm industries. That means that a full 32 percent, or one-third, of Ohioans worked in government-dependent industries in 2010.

Even the most liberal-progressive proponent of big government must concede that for big government to exist, the state must first have a vibrant private sector that generates tax revenues to fund big government. In Ohio, we've had big government, but lacked a vibrant private sector. This imbalance has led to deficits and looming fiscal crises in local governments across Ohio.

For Ohio's private sector to fully recover to its March 2000 population adjusted mark of 42.6 percent, it would have to reach 4,914,551 jobs, or 542,051 more jobs than Ohio has today. Keep in mind that during the booming 1990s, Ohio added 713,600 private sector jobs. No serious expert expects the American economy to add jobs at the pace set in the 1990s. Thus, based on analyzing historical trend data of Ohio job growth, the realistic date Ohio likely will reach a full recovery in its job market is November 2021—roughly coinciding with the 21st birthday of a child born in March of 2000.

According to the Fraser Institute's Economic Freedom of North America Annual Report in 2011, Ohio's economic freedom is low compared to other states. The Fraser Institute report analyzes economic data such as general consumption expenditures by government as a percentage of Gross Domestic Product (GDP) and government employment as a percentage of total state employment to determine the overall economic freedom of each jurisdiction. Overall Ohio is ranked as the 44th economically freest state. In the three areas ranked, Ohio is the worst ranked for size of government, the 31st ranked for takings and discriminatory taxes, and 39th ranked for labor market freedom. Consistent with the growth of Ohio government, Ohio's general consumption expenditures by government as a percentage of GDP went from 9.9 percent in 1981 to 15 percent in 2009.

The Land of Titans

One hundred years ago, the titans of industry and leaders of innovation included many Ohioans and Ohio companies. These men and their companies drove (in some cases, literally) the American economy. These people or companies were household names in America and some still are today.

- Henry Crowell and the Quaker Oats Company (1901)
- Harvey Firestone and the Firestone Tire and Rubber Company (1900)
- Charles Kettering and Delco (1909)
- Bernard H. Kroger and the Kroger's Food Stores (1883)
- George H. Mead and Mead Paper Company (1882)
- John H. Patterson and National Cash Register (NCR) Company (1884)
- William C. Procter and the Procter & Gamble Company (1837)
- John D. Rockefeller and the Standard Oil Company (1870)
- Orville and Wilbur Wright (1903)

The very fact that many of these companies are still industry leaders gives testament to the sheer power of those companies to change and innovate.

Over the last few decades, the names and companies coming out of Ohio—again, names many Americans would recognize—are few and far between. The only Ohio companies making the Fortune 100 list in 2012 were Cardinal Health (#21), Kroger (#23), Procter & Gamble (#27), Marathon Petroleum (#31), and Nationwide (#100). There is Rubbermaid and IAMS dog food from the 1980s. Though a giant in Ohio, surprisingly, Les Wexner is not a household name outside of Ohio and New York City, though the companies he created (Limited Brands; Victoria Secret; Abercrombie & Fitch; Bath & Body Works; etc.) certainly are easily recognizable. The J.M. Smuckers Company and Wendy's also fall into this category of being known. Like Kroger, Nationwide, and Procter & Gamble, these two companies began well before the 1980s.

Marathon Petroleum is a new entrant to the Fortune 100 list after being spun-off from Houston-based Marathon Oil in June 2011. Marathon Oil began in 1887 as The Ohio Oil Company. John D. Rockefeller and Standard Oil acquired it in 1889. The precursor company to Marathon Oil came out of the federal government break-up of Standard Oil.

Of course, there are many good companies in Ohio that provide thousands of jobs and, in some cases, serve as industry leaders engaging in innovative work within their fields. Some of these companies started decades ago. These companies include Ariel Corporation (compressors), Cintas Corporation (uniforms), Ohio Arts (toys), and the Timken Corporation (bearings).

Today, the titans of American industry and the leading companies come, not from Ohio, but, like modern U.S. presidents, from states to the South and West. These individuals and/or their companies are truly household names:

- Jeff Bezos and Amazon (Washington)
- Michael Dell and Dell Computer Corporation (Texas)
- Bill Gates and Microsoft (Washington)
- Andrew Grove and Intel (California)
- Steve Jobs and Apple (California)
- John Mackey and Whole Foods Market (Texas)
- Larry Page and Sergei Brin and Google (California)
- Howard Schultz and Starbucks (Washington)
- Fred Smith and FedEx (Tennessee)
- Sam Walton and Wal-mart Corporation (Arkansas)
- Mark Zuckerberg and Facebook (California)

Sure, some of these companies started years ago, but these companies dominate the American psyche today. Other than Sam Walton, these men have dominated the global economy over the last two decades.

Whether it is presidents, job growth, or leaders of industry, Ohio isn't leading the pack. So, what happened to Ohio over the last 100 years to go from national leader to national laggard?

A Lack of Vision or the Wrong Vision

From 1963 to 2001, Ohio's Republican and Democratic governors lacked the vision to put in place reforms that would be bearing fruit today, or, worse, had the wrong vision. James Rhodes' four terms earned him naming rights to the tallest (government) building in Columbus, but his legacy is instituting the city income tax in Columbus as mayor and laying the foundation for the state income tax. John Gilligan implemented the state income tax.

Richard Celeste's vision and eight years in office resulted in sticking us with the high cost of public sector collective bargaining and the entrenched power of labor unions. George Voinovich served two terms as governor where he raised taxes and increased spending, but he is more well known for his moderate U.S. Senate career than for his time as governor.

It is too early to determine the lasting positive or negative impact, if any, of Bob Taft (more spending and the Deferred Retirement Option Plan pension program, but business tax reform), Ted Strickland (more unionization and a failure to act), and John Kasich (the early signs are troubling).

These men were good, hardworking governors, but none of them had the vision to put in place the policies that would allow Ohio to be competitive in a global marketplace and serve as an incubator for entrepreneurs. Even worse, Governor Celeste's actions made Ohio less competitive due to the need for higher taxes to fund the gold-plated government compensation packages that have built up since he rammed through the public sector collective bargaining law in 1983.

When experts talk about great governors who instituted lasting, game-changing reform in the United States, these men don't make the list. Think Governor Tommy Thompson's Wisconsin Works welfare reforms in 1996 that became the model for national welfare reforms or Governor Jeb Bush's A+ Plan education reform in Florida in 1999 that dramatically improved Florida's K-12 educational outcomes and is used as the model in other states. More recently, Wisconsin Governor Scott Walker's government collective bargaining reforms in 2011 spurred a national movement in other states to realign government compensation packages to the economic realities of today.

For far too long, Ohio has been a follower, implementing reforms long after other states have led the way. By the time Ohio adopts the reforms, other states have already moved on to the next series of reforms. Part of the reason for this laggard reputation is Ohio's heavy reliance on what Walter Russell Mead refers to as the blue social model. The blue social model is the socio-economic model that arose during the New Deal era that resulted in a bureaucratic way of life in America.

As Mead writes in "Why Blue Can't Save the Inner Cities Part I" on his *ViaMeadia* blog:

> In the peak years of the blue social model (roughly, FDR through Ronald Reagan, or 1933 through 1984), American economic life was bureaucratic. Kids went to schools where they learned to sit at a desk and do what they were told. Those who learned the basics and graduated from high school worked in factories. Those who did better and got a bachelor's degree worked in offices. Those who did better still and went on to graduate school moved into the professions.

> Once employed, people moved gradually up the ranks or the salary scale based on seniority and paper credentials. Get a master's degree and get a salary bump. Accumulate seniority and get the best assignments. At the end, everybody retires at the mandatory retirement age and collects a defined benefits pension until the final checkout comes.

> The whole economy didn't work this way. There were still holdovers from the old, pre-organized world: sharecroppers, Coney Island carnival barkers, unfranchised Mom and Pop burger joints and so on. There were also entrepreneurs and start ups and sales-oriented companies where the bottom line mattered more than credentials and procedures. But more than before or since, the Age of Blue was a time when the organized and predictable corporate-bureaucratic world dominated American culture and life.

During the Blue Age, life in government was not very different from life outside it. Salaries were a bit lower and the bureaucratic structures were sometimes more rigid, but on the whole post office clerks and insurance company clerks had similar work experiences and their families lived similar lives.

As this social model increasingly broke up in the 1980s, conditions in the private and public sector diverged. Automation reduced the number of clerical positions in the insurance industry, but politics slowed the pace of change in the Post Office. Private sector employment changed its nature, becoming less predictable, less egalitarian (in terms of salary distribution), and companies shifted from defined benefit pensions based on seniority to defined contribution benefits based on how much employees paid in.

Generally, political inertia and public worker unions combined to keep government in the Blue Age even as the rest of the economy moved on. Today, the experiences and the expectations of people in the private sector and people in the public sector are quite different.

Mead identifies three key crises in the blue social model in "American Challenges: The Blue Model Breaks Down":

The first is the government's role in providing the benefits associated with the blue system. When we talk about 'runaway entitlement programs' today we are talking about commitments by the government to provide retirement and other social benefits that originated as part of the blue system social contract. Workers could retire as early as 62 with a combination of Social Security, private pensions and, as of the 1960s, Medicare coverage. These costs are now exploding and it is clear that the government can't pay them into the future.

The second crisis is that the government is now the last true-blue employer in the country. Federal, state and local governments are often staffed by lifetime civil servants, whose jobs are protected by law and by some of the last truly powerful unions in the country. That means it is incredibly expensive for governments to do anything at all, and they are poorly equipped to respond nimbly to the fast-changing conditions of America today. The cost problem is aggravated because quasi-governmental sectors of the economy (like the health and university industries) are also by and large pretty blue: high wages, stable employment, cumbersome procedures — and powerful unions.

Government is simply too unproductive, too unresponsive and too expensive to do what needs to be done at a reasonable cost. (Government also still has the anti-consumer mentality of the old blue monopolies: if you don't like the crappy services government provides — move.) Public schools are increasingly expensive to run, and yet they do not provide improved services to match those exploding costs.

Finally, culturally and intellectually, bureaucrats and politicians often remain blue. That is, they think instinctively in the old ways, come up with blue solutions to non-blue problems, and often fail to grasp either the constraints or the opportunities of the new era.

Ohio, as vividly illustrated by the fight and union victory on collective bargaining reform in 2011, is stuck in the blue social model.

Part of Ohio's challenge is that its ties to organized labor run far deeper than most states. Therefore, shaking off the yoke of unionism will be that much harder. For example, according to Barry T. Hirsch in "Sluggish Institutions in a Dynamic World: Can Unions and Industrial Competition Coexist?," the concentration of the domestic car industry in the late 1970s was second greatest in Ohio (Michigan was first), which came hand in hand with labor unions. In all likelihood, as the battle over collective bargaining reform showed, Ohio will be among the last states to truly break from the blue social model.

This blue social model has resulted in Ohio having the 18th highest burden of state and local taxes and the seventh highest number of taxing government entities in America. Reducing the tax burden and number of taxing entities will be enormously difficult, but Ohio cannot escape the blue social model without tackling these issues.

Even when Republicans gained power, state spending went up, and the necessary budgetary realignment failed to occur. From 1990 through 2013 (through Governor Kasich's 2012-2013 state budget), state general revenue fund expenditures will have gone up by 148 percent or 44 percent after adjusting for inflation. That means general revenue fund expenditures exceeded inflation by 2 percent every year on average over the last 22 years. Republicans controlled the Governor's Office and the General Assembly during most of these years. Had Ohio's elected officials held general revenue fund expenditures to inflation plus population growth, the state budget would be less than $22 billion today (versus $27 billion).

Whether intentional or not, Governor Kasich spent his first year in office taking actions that undermined the conservative movement. First, in justifying high salaries for some of his top staffers, he noted to reporters that he had to pay high wages to compete against the private sector. The idea that someone would only serve in government if he could match or surpass private sector pay or that government must pay top dollar to attract the best candidates are ideas promoted by liberal-progressive think tanks and politicians. In fact, opponents of the government collective bargaining reforms contained in Senate Bill 5 made just these points when justifying the gold-plated compensation packages of government workers.

I don't make this criticism in a vacuum. When the Buckeye Institute offered me the president's job, they offered me the same $125,000 salary and paid parking benefit that my predecessor had received. Prior to accepting, I analyzed the financial records and discovered that the Buckeye Institute, much like the state of Ohio, was a fiscal mess. It had roughly $430,000 in liabilities, bills more than a year overdue, and less than $5,000 cash on hand. I informed the Board of Trustees about my findings and indicated to them that they could not afford to pay me the salary they had offered. I offered to take a substantial pay-cut down to $83,000 and pay my own parking costs with the understanding that, if I turned around the Buckeye Institute, the Board of Trustees would reward me accordingly.

Upon arrival, I cut the pay of other staffers to reflect the fiscal reality under which we were operating. Like me, they weren't at the Buckeye Institute to get rich. They believed in what we were trying to do.

When I left the Buckeye Institute roughly two and a half years later on December 31, 2011, it had over $200,000 cash on hand, it was debt free, it had a record number of new donors, and it had more credibility and relevance than at any time in its 22 year history. I never had the Buckeye Institute pay for my parking costs and received only one raise in late 2010 that increased my yearly pay to $110,000. I don't tell you this information out of self-promotion. I did what anyone in my shoes would have done. I tell you this information because it is the same mindset that politicians and political appointees should always bring to their government work, especially conservatives.

Then, facing an estimated $8 billion deficit, Governor Kasich's budget increases general revenue fund expenditures over the next two years, instead of taking the opportunity to realign state spending and rejecting the unjustifiable spending increases of the previous two decades. This failure in facing an unprecedented crisis indicated that he does not believe Ohio's state budget was fundamentally out-of-whack.

Next, one of Governor Kasich's top priorities outside of the budget is his opaque JobsOhio program, which like the Third Frontier grant program reflects blue social model thinking in that it looks to government as the source of increased prosperity. Despite the abhorrent track record of government agencies (quasi or not) picking winners and losers (see federal and state green energy investments), Governor Kasich appears to believe that JobsOhio will deftly invest taxpayers' resources in a manner that avoids corporate rent seeking.

The similarity between Governor Kasich's JobsOhio program and President Obama's jobs plan has not been lost on those analyzing both efforts. As detailed in "A Republican Governor's Obama-like Jobs Plan" in *Fortune*:

> Kasich is in the midst of implementing a sweeping job-creation strategy much more ideologically akin to Obama's then Romney's. An iconoclastic, even populist, leader often confused for a conservative hardliner, Kasich is pushing as the centerpiece of his governorship a recovery plan that calls for aggressive government intervention in the market…If it sounds like industrial policy—in which the state chooses private-sector winners and losers, an approach conservative economists deride as anti-free market— that's largely because it is.

The article then highlights JobsOhio head Mark Kvamme's defense of President Obama's Solyndra loan by noting his view that "Republicans were wrong to vilify the White House for the company's failure." Kvamme even noted interest in investing in Solyndra.

Through JobsOhio, Governor Kasich also plays the destructive game of seeing which state can spend the most money to keep and attract companies instead of working to improve the overall business environment by lowering state and local taxes, driving aggressive regulatory reforms, and instituting workplace freedom for Ohio workers and their employers. Even if used effectively during his term, just like Medicaid Part D, RomneyCare, and other government programs created by Republicans, other politicians likely will eliminate the positive components of JobsOhio and turn it into a stimulus-like program that helps their entrenched interests, but does little for taxpayers.

Because of state budget cuts, Governor Kasich spent his first year in office telling local governments that they had to tighten their belts by reducing costs. Yet, state government workers who already make 28 percent more than their private sector neighbors received $21 million worth of yearly raises under the most recent union contract approved by Governor Kasich. Apparently what is good for the goose is not good for the gander in Ohio. These high and ever increasing compensation costs have led to the perilous fiscal condition of Ohio's five government pensions, which could require a taxpayer bailout.

To make matters worse, even before the state budget cuts, local governments were already under financial duress. For example, according to their October 2010 five-year projections to the Ohio Department of Education, Ohio's school districts projected a collective deficit of $7.6 billion by 2015, with compensation package costs swallowing 96 percent of all projected revenues. Roughly a year and a half later, in the May 2012 five-year projections, those same school districts increased their tax revenue projections by over $2.1 billion as compared to the October 2010 projections. Given the declining value of homes as announced in 2011 by county auditors, Ohioans cannot afford multi-billion tax hikes. With 57 percent of new levies and hundreds of other local taxes being approved in the last year, the total tax burden on Ohioans has gone up under Governor Kasich. So, his claim to have eliminated the $8 billion state budget deficit without raising taxes is a bit misleading given that his enormous cuts to local governments – funds he used to eliminate the deficit – resulted in those entities raising taxes.

On taxes, though he takes credit now, his proposed 2012-2013 budget did not contain the repeal of Ohio's estate tax. In fact, nowhere in his 17-page 2011 State of the State remarks did Governor Kasich even mention the repeal of the estate tax. Conservatives in the legislature inserted that tax cut into the budget bill. There were efforts to remove the estate tax repeal language from the budget bill, but that effort failed when grassroots Ohioans who had been working for several years to put an initiative on the ballot exerted enormous pressure on legislators to keep their word or face a ballot initiative.

Finally, Governor Kasich does not support a workplace freedom law. Contrary to media reports, those individuals trying to put a workplace freedom initiative on the ballot do not want Governor Kasich involved in any way with the effort due to his toxicity with voters and low approval ratings. After Governor Kasich's team committed to stay neutral, he has actively worked to undermine the efforts of Ohioans for Workplace Freedom, the grassroots group working to allow Ohioans to vote on the issue, by calling potential donors to get them to cease their support of this critical effort. A workplace freedom law would allow Ohio companies to compete with businesses in the South and West of the U.S., including newly free Indiana, and give workers the right to choose for themselves whether to join labor unions. No single other policy change in Ohio would have a more significant impact than implementing a workplace freedom law.

The bottom line is that Ohio has been an economic laggard for decades and is poised to continue on that path. This must change. To reform Ohio's economy, you must first understand how the current political system is failing us.

2

THE POLITICAL SYSTEM DOESN'T WORK

Ohio Legislator: "I think we should let OPERS [the state government pension system] *invest the private funds of taxpayers."*

No matter how politicians want to cut it, Ohio's health is dependent upon a vibrant economy that creates private sector jobs. Big government liberal-progressives need a strong private sector to funnel tax revenues to their government programs. Small government conservative-libertarians need a strong private sector to keep taxes in check. Based on Ohio's poor job growth over the last two decades, the politicians we elected failed to put in place policies to ignite the economic engine in Ohio.

The above words, spoken by an elected official deemed to be a fiscal conservative, reflect one of the many problems with Ohio's political system, especially considering that the Ohio Public Employee Retirement System is only funded 75 cents for every $1.00 in liabilities due to poor investment decisions. Those results are only achievable using misleading government accounting rules not available for private sector pension plans. The reality is that for many elected officials, their political jobs are the best, most lucrative jobs they have or will ever have. This is true especially when the financial benefit from receiving defined benefit retirement plans is added to their compensation packages.

In fact, as the *Dispatch* reported on October 31, 2010, fifteen legislators in the Ohio House and Senate collect government pensions making them double dippers. The *Dispatch* noted that 54 legislators either receive government pensions and/or have household family members who receive government pensions. How many of these men and women have the courage to substantially reduce the government pensions for future retirees when Ohioans know of the gold-plated pensions they currently receive?

The answer is very few given that the pension reform legislation introduced in May of 2012 and passed by the Ohio Senate consists merely of minor changes proposed by the five government pensions. On June 5, 2012, even voters in heavily Democratic California passed government pensions reforms. Specifically, in San Diego and San Jose, voters overwhelmingly passed propositions that make more significant changes to the city pension plans than Ohio's Republican-controlled legislature is willing to do.

Being a politician or working for a politician has never been more lucrative in Ohio. For example, Joyce Beatty could receive a government pension north of $200,000 per year because President Gordon Gee quadrupled her government salary at Ohio State for three years. This pension could be in addition to her soon-to-be congressional salary. These are not isolated incidences. There are dozens of double dippers in the General Assembly and in the cabinet of Governor Kasich. It is highly doubtful these gold-plated financial outcomes would have occurred had these men and women spent their careers in the private sector. As a point of reference, to receive a $200,000 annual pension in retirement, a private sector Ohioan would have to have roughly $3,000,000 in the bank by the age of sixty.

For example, at a meeting in 2010, one elected official boldly proclaimed that he could easily make a lot more in the private sector. Beyond the sheer chutzpah of making such a claim during one of the worst economic times in modern history, the claim is total puffery. It is a claim easily uttered, but impossible to prove. Outside of becoming a highly-paid lobbyist, which he could only do because of his career in politics, the politician's thin background makes it highly unlikely that, given Ohio's horrible economy, he would have surpassed the total compensation package he has received in politics, including a pension.

If politicians showed a little more gratitude for how good they have it, then perhaps Ohioans would think better of them. With such an appealing compensation package, it isn't surprising that so many people seek office and fight hard to stay there. Yet, using Ohio's job record as the metric of success, these politicians have failed us over the last two decades.

Term Limits Is Not the Problem

Please see: Congress, United States. Enough said.

It is staggering that the same pundits (and lobbyists) who blame term limits for the dysfunction in Ohio's General Assembly conveniently ignore the same dysfunction in the U.S. Congress. One would think that dysfunction occurring in similar political entities where one entity has term limits and the other does not would result in the dismissal of term limits as the culprit of the dysfunction.

With 66 percent of the vote, Ohioans wisely and unequivocally passed term limits in 1992 to curb the number of career politicians in the state legislature. The power amassed by career politicians simply became too great, as demonstrated by the career of Ohio House Speaker Vern Riffe. Unfortunately for Ohioans, term limits did not have the impact expected because politicians figured out ways to circumvent the term limits.

Most notably, current Speaker William Batchelder first began serving in the legislature in the 1960s. After he was term limited out of the Ohio House in 2000, he spent a few years as a judge and then promptly jumped back into the Ohio House in 2007. Speaker Batchelder isn't the only member of the General Assembly with such a long history of service.

In fact, based on the actual data, term limits did not result in a General Assembly with little experience in it. To see if term limits (i.e., inexperience) is indeed to blame for Ohio's legislative ills, I looked at the legislative experience by legislator and General Assembly for five different terms: 1971-1972, 1981-1982, 1991-1992 (the last one before term limits), 2001-2001, and 2011-2012 (the current one). The average years of experience for legislators for those terms are 4.16, 7.41, 9.36, 4.24, and 6.54, respectively. Term limits cut the average term by more than half just ten years later.

After term limits, as some have correctly noted, those wily politicians began the practice of jumping back and forth and back between the House and Senate. This bouncing practice resulted in the average term rising by 54 percent over the last ten years. The average term now is only 12 percent less than the average term in the halcyon days of 1981-1982 (ironically, just before the partisan passage of Ohio's collective bargaining law).

In terms of institutional experience, the total years of experience over those five terms totaled 549, 978, 1,235, 560, and 863. Again, the total years of experience today is only 12 percent less than the total experience in 1981-1982. So much for inexperience being responsible for today's Statehouse ills.

A closer look shows yet another surprise. Over those five terms, the number of legislators with 30 years or more of experience was 0, 2, 1, 0, and 4. Those with 20 years or more totaled 2, 5, 14, 2, and 14. This means there are as many seasoned veterans today than in the year before the term limits amendment passed.

Perhaps something else is to blame for Ohio's legislative ills. A more likely cause of legislative dysfunction is the aggressive actions taken by both the Republican and Democratic parties to handpick candidates and involve themselves in primaries to insure their candidates win. This practice breeds extreme loyalty to the parties and their leadership, but leaves people on Main Street in the backseat. Reelection campaigns for incumbents are run and funded by the party caucuses. Bucking the party results in a loss of reelection funds.

As for the issue of legislators not knowing how things work because term limits prevents them from gaining the experience to navigate the system, either we've made the system too complex or we are sending the wrong people to Columbus. If eight years really isn't enough time to learn the rules and get some things done, then we need to reform how the General Assembly works. Remember, there are 14 legislators in the General Assembly with 20 years or more of experience. Certainly, these veterans can provide whatever institutional memory is needed to get the ball rolling. A child who cannot read, write, or do math will enter and exit elementary and middle school knowing algebra and chemistry in eight years. Can't we expect similar progress from our legislators?

It is time to stop blaming term limits and find a better explanation for Ohio's political problems.

System Rewards Maintaining the Status Quo

The issue isn't really "who" is in the Statehouse and whether those individuals have decades of experience under their belts. The real issue, lost in the kerfuffle over term limits, is who "controls" the Statehouse, and I don't mean which political party. On this count, it is clear that over the last few decades as government and opportunities to make money from government grew, party bosses and their entrenched allies increasingly have controlled the Statehouse.

After all, does anyone really believe that more experience would result in better policy outcomes? The systemic failure to put in place the right policies in the 1970s, 1980s, and 1990s to ensure Ohio's economy provided widespread opportunities for Ohioans undermines that notion. Think about that statement. Ohio is an economic mess. It has gone from one of America's best economies to one of its worst over the last 22 years (5th worst). If the system before term limits was so great, why didn't it result in policies that allowed Ohio to excel more rapidly than other states in the good times (38th in job growth during the 1990s) and crash less severely in the bad times (2nd in job losses in the 2000s)?

If fact, just the opposite occurred in the days before term limits. When Democrats controlled the levers of power under legendary Speaker Riffe and Governor Celeste in 1983, they rammed through Ohio's pro-union collective bargaining law. That law, far more than any other piece of legislation, is responsible for the ever-increasing compensation package costs of government, especially at the local level. You may support those high costs and believe taxpayers should foot the bill no matter how high those costs rise, but it is indisputable that public sector collective bargaining drove Ohio's state and local tax burden from among the lowest in the country to among the highest.

Even the most right or left wing legislators are constrained by their party. Legislation does not get introduced, let alone passed, if party and statewide leaders don't want it. The most recent examples are the "Heartbeat" bill that regulates when a woman can have an abortion (stalled in the Senate) and workplace freedom legislation that would give Ohioans the right to choose whether to join labor unions (not even introduced). That has been the case for far longer than term limits have been in place.

The system today is one in which the party leaders control who runs for office (or receives a vacancy appointment) and which pieces of legislation make it out of the legislature. Parties endorse candidates in primaries and then do all that they can do to eliminate primaries or guarantee their endorsed candidate prevails. As a result, legislators are indebted to the political party and leadership for their jobs and dependent upon them for reelection support.

This system, therefore, leads to the outcome you would expect when party control matters more than implementing the right policies. It frankly doesn't matter who is actually elected. The outcome is one in which timidity of action and nibbling around the margins of big issues predominates. The focus is on doing enough to claim the mantle of reform, but not too much so that the next election is at risk. It is a status quo system.

This timidity and nibbling is evident when looking at how elected officials deal with the pay and pensions of government workers. Despite the proposed reforms in <u>future</u> pay scales (step increases and longevity) in Senate Bill 5 (the rare exception on going big), no piece of that legislation dealt with the existing base pay of government workers (state or local). Without realigning base pay, the only outcome for many government entities is either increasing taxes or cutting programs and staff.

Over the last few years, many Ohioans in the private sector have experienced pay cuts and job losses. Even unionized workers have had to give up base pay in Ohio. Yet, with the exception of a handful of government entities, base pay reductions aren't even part of the discussion.

At the state level, Governor Kasich came into office facing a budgetary deficit of roughly $8 billion. As the Buckeye Institute report "The Grand Bargain is Dead: The Compensation of State Government Workers Far Exceeds Their Private-Sector Neighbors" found, the compensation packages of state government workers are 28 percent higher than their private sector neighbors. Did Governor Kasich boldly declare "exigent circumstances" due to an historic deficit and reduce the base pay of state workers as part of balancing the budget? No. Even Toledo Mayor Mike Bell had the courage to declare "exigent circumstances" to deal with his deficit and the State Employment Relations Board upheld his right to do so. Governor Kasich did nothing to rein in existing personnel costs.

Even worse, Governor Kasich negotiated a new contract with the government unions that <u>increased</u> government pay cost by $21 million per year. So, not only did taxpayers not get any relief once the Senate

Bill 5 reforms were repealed, but their costs actually went up. Governor Kasich negotiated this deal after lecturing local governments to cut costs without raising taxes following his budget cuts in 2011. The largest cost in local governments is compensation packages. Because of the budget cuts, local governments now must do at the local level what Governor Kasich refused to do at the state level. As noted below, because local governments also won't tackle this growing cost problem, Ohioans can expect local taxes to go up.

To properly define the problem, one only has to look at the fiscal conditions of Ohio school districts. Based on the most recent financial data submitted by the school districts to the Ohio Department of Education in May 2012, by 2016, Ohio's school districts will require nearly $2.2 billion in additional property tax revenue. Even with that additional tax burden, the school districts still project a statewide deficit of roughly $2.8 billion in 2016, which is $4.8 billion lower than the October 2010 deficit projection. The $4.8 billion additional deficit literally just disappeared.

To accomplish this major "turnaround," the school districts project they will hold compensation package growth to just 6.11 percent over six years, or just over 1 percent per year. Such a low growth rate over a six-year period would be a miracle. Because the projections are not legally binding, it is more likely that the school districts held the compensation package increases so low to make sure that their 2016 projected ending cash balance reflected a small deficit or even a surplus.

Of the $4.8 billion reduction from the October 2010 deficit projections, 89 percent of it is the difference between the October 2010 compensation package projections that reflected more than 19 percent growth and the May 2012 compensation package projections that hold growth to just 6.11 percent. Why would the school districts make such unrealistic projections? Two reasons: first, after the October 2010 projections, the Buckeye Institute developed easy-to-understand one page sheets on every school district that highlighted the five-year projections and the savings that could be realized by making reasonable compensation package reductions. Ohioans used these one-pagers extensively to defeat levies and raise questions with school district administrators and board members. School districts don't want to see those one-pagers again.

The second more important reason is that school districts know that voters are in no mood to increase taxes in such tough times. We are living in an age of austerity. If school districts, however, show voters via the five-year projections that they allegedly made the tough decisions and that the projected fiscal conditions of the school districts have magically improved, they can more reasonably argue that remaining deficits should be eliminated by raising property taxes. You can count on two outcomes: taxes will go up and compensation package costs will not be held over the next six years to just 6.11 percent.

We know based on the last 20 years, raising taxes is always the choice selected by school districts. They only cut programs and staff as a threat to get residents to raise taxes. As for realigning compensation packages, it is so rare it never enters the conversation.

With Governor Kasich's belief that government should pay salaries at a level competitive with the private sector, this unfortunate and costly outcome is not a surprise. Public service, especially for political appointees, is supposed to be sacrificial; meaning, you sacrifice private sector pay to serve a larger cause. For bureaucrats, you give up higher pay in the private sector for job security and a decent pension (i.e., the grand bargain between taxpayers and government workers). Today, both political appointees and bureaucrats get gold-plated pay and benefits largely non-existent in the private sector.

Over the last two decades, compensation package increases in state and local governments across Ohio have outpaced inflation year after year. As Ohio's private sector cratered in the last decade, the ability of taxpayers to fund those high compensation costs has become untenable.

Here is a vital fact: the size of government measured by employees in Ohio today is roughly the same as it was in 2000, with the financial cost having exceeded inflation in most of those years. At the same time, the number of private sector workers generating tax revenue to support government has declined by roughly 500,000 workers. The answer is not to increase the tax burden on those Ohioans still possessing jobs. The answer is to reduce spending.

When it comes to reforming government pensions, the timidity and nibbling is worse. One of the reasons is because so many legislators are either double dippers (receiving both a government pension check and a salary check each month) or are rapidly accumulating their years of service, and thus they have a direct and lucrative financial stake in maintaining the status quo. Minor changes won't have much of a lasting impact on legislators' retirement incomes.

For example, according to the Buckeye Institute state salary data tool, a Nurse I in the Department of Rehabilitations and Corrections earned roughly $200,000 each year from 2003 to 2005 due to more than doubling his base salary with overtime. Under the current pension formula, he would receive a starting pension of $132,041 per year after thirty years of service. With the 3 percent guaranteed cost of living adjustment, assuming he received the government pension for 18 years, his payout would be $2,982,804. This example is not meant to disparage that worker, as he is doing what anyone would do for his family facing a similar compensation system.

Tweaking the pension formula to reflect the average of the highest five years (instead of three), which is one of the "reform" proposals of the government pensions, would drag his average salary down to $182,330. The result is that his first year pension would decrease by only $12,000 and his lifetime payout would drop by just $260,000. These savings are small and won't help the five government pensions that already are fiscally underwater right the ship or reduce the growing bailout risk for taxpayers by much.

Real reforms as outlined in both Buckeye Institute reports "The Grand Bargain" and "Hanging by a Thread: Big Payouts and Promises Leave Ohio Pension Plans on the Brink of Collapse—or a Massive Bailout" would ensure taxpayers would not be on the hook for a bailout. These reforms include the following: a shift to a defined contribution system like Michigan did in 1997 or a shift to a true hybrid system (a defined benefit system capped with remaining benefit flowing into a defined contribution system) like Democratic-led Rhode Island did in 2011, using career salary averages without add-ins such as overtime to determine the pension, and reducing the cost of living adjustment (COLA) to the Social Security COLA. Such reforms, however, also would significantly lower the pensions of government retirees, including politicians, to reflect those retirements common in the private sector in Ohio.

The prevalence of double dippers in the legislature and Governor Kasich's cabinet demonstrates another fundamental problem. These individuals became double dippers because of spending their careers in government. In some cases, these individuals served in previous Republican majorities or administrations and, as detailed in this book, didn't push for key reforms in their first at bat. Why does anyone believe they will knock it out of the park this time? Timidity is an inherent quality in a political system that produces double dippers. If Ohioans want innovation, they must "hire" innovators from outside the political system.

The system we have in Ohio works well for politicians, government workers, and lobbyists. It is a miserable failure for taxpayers and is clearly unsustainable.

Local Politicians Rarely Cut Taxes

Why is it that local taxes rarely, if ever, get cut? Whether it is our property taxes, city income taxes, county sales taxes, or other local taxes, rates climb and there is little debate about reducing taxes. Ever wondered why that is the case? Human nature and labor unions are the reasons.

First, people at work and in their communities abhor interpersonal conflict and must possess a motive to work against that ingrained desire to get along. In the private sector, the motive is profit, which determines pay and job security. In government, no such motive exists, which is precisely why even pro-union politicians like President Franklin D. Roosevelt opposed giving government workers the entitlement to collectively bargain.

Without the necessary motive to work against their desire to get along, when collective bargaining negotiations occur between government unions and government entities, government managers—risk averse by the fact they work in government—don't engage in the conflict necessary to keep a lid on compensation packages. Since compensation packages swallow the vast majority of local budgets, keeping spending down and taxes low requires restraining the growth of compensation packages of government workers. With no motive to counter the desire to get along, few government entities restrain compensation package costs.

Second, the power of government unions further exacerbates the issue. By actively getting involved in local elections, government unions can increase the likelihood that the people with whom they will negotiate a contract are "their" people. Government unions also can bring to bear enormous resources to maintain the status quo. These resources range from the $42 million in funds poured into the campaign to reverse the collective bargaining reforms contained in Senate Bill 5 in 2011 to the skilled union negotiation employees who, unlike their government counterparts, engage in many contract negotiations across Ohio in a year, thereby gaining valuable experience. Taxpayers are ill equipped to counter union money and experience.

Even more insidious are the campaign contributions from those who stand to gain financially from the tax increases, especially government vendors. Government vendors contribute heavily to local tax hike campaigns, thereby ensuring their government clients have the money to pay their contracts. This activity is as close to pay to play as you can get.

For example, in the most recent levy campaign for Dublin City Schools, according to the campaign finance reports at the Franklin County Board of Elections, the Good Schools Committee raised $64,729 for the property tax levy-bond campaign. Of that amount, $46,392—a full 72 percent—came from vendors and employees (most of the funds came from vendors). According to the list of vendors from Dublin City Schools for 2010-2011, the vendors who supported the levy increase received payments from the district totaling over $12 million. Based on this data, it is patently false for school districts to claim that taxpayers, rather than vendors, support the levy increase.

Not surprisingly, several of the school district's vendors also did work for the Good Schools Committee, including Hopkins Printing, Avakian Consulting, and Rich & Gillis Law Group. Not counting the indirect free media from the weekly newspapers and the actions done by the school district in support of the levy campaign, the Good Schools Committee spent over $41,000 on the levy campaign. Good government proponents rightfully argue that it is relevant how much special interests give to politicians. It is equally relevant how much government vendors give to tax increase campaigns.

[JINO Alert #1: Media outlets should get this information and publish pieces highlighting this conflict of interest.]

Though Dublin voters rejected the levy this time, the odds, as discussed in Chapter 7, are against taxpayers. Without the ability to take campaign funds from vendors and employees, opponents of local tax increases don't stand a chance in the long run. As a result, taxes always tend to go up.

Taxes certainly never go down.

The City of Dublin provides a great example of the problem. Because of the number of businesses in Dublin, the size of the city explodes during the workweek as workers from around Central Ohio enter the city. The city income tax of 2 percent is collected on all of those workers, many of whom don't live in Dublin. This allows Dublin to pocket city income taxes because the city does not have to provide residential services to those workers.

As a result, Dublin has an enormous rainy day fund. Even during the economic downturn, Dublin grew its rainy day fund from roughly 75 percent of a full year's budget to 85 percent of a full year's budget. That means that Dublin could waive city incomes taxes for a full year and still cover 85 percent of all costs. This strong financial position calls for a tax reduction to provide residents with a fiscal break and to create a more competitive business environment for companies. With Columbus raising its income tax rate to 2.5 percent, Dublin could attract more companies to move to its jurisdiction.

Yet, in the recent campaign for city council, all of the candidates for city council rejected the idea of a tax cut. One has to wonder how big a rainy day fund will be needed before Dublin's elected officials realize that Ohioans who live and work in the city should be able to keep more of their hard earned salaries. Until then, Dublin will buy more outdoor art, build more roundabouts, and construct fancy commercial buildings like the BriHi development in Historic Dublin that came in way over budget, lacks adequate parking, and fails to attract a full contingent of occupants.

Ironically, while the city of Dublin is flush with tax revenue,

Dublin City Schools has to make cuts. Neither entity is a paragon of fiscal restraint; rather, both entities spend too much money. The difference is that the city benefits from corporate headquarters. If government leaders would think outside the box, they could present taxpayers with a proposition that could help the city, the school district, taxpayers, and the private sector.

For example, if the city agreed to a 0.25 percent income tax cut and the school district requested a 0.15 percent income tax increase, then taxpayers would see a net reduction in local taxes. Assume the city receives $71.6 million per year based on the current 2 percent income tax on roughly $3.58 billion in income. A 0.25 percent reduction would "cost" the city $8.95 million. The school district's 0.15 percent income tax would add $5.37 million to its coffers. Taxpayers would keep $3.58 million to spend as they see fit, and companies would be more attractive to potential workers due to the lower personal tax burden.

The city would still receive enough revenue to responsibly operate and, with the lower income tax rate, become even more competitive vis-à-vis the other cities in Central Ohio that are raising their rates. The school district would diversify its tax base and bring in revenue allowing it to keep a lid on property tax increases. Of course, taxpayers should reject any deal unless base compensation reductions occurred in both the city and school district. This type of deal is possible in suburban jurisdictions across Ohio.

This system—from the state level down to how local property tax levy campaigns are funded—must be reformed to give more power to citizens and less power to bureaucrats and special interest groups. All too often, the political system produces politicians who focus on the wrong problems or who make things worse. Taxpayers are left paying the bill for failures produced by Ohio's political system.

3

THE TENDENCY TO FOCUS ON THE WRONG PROBLEMS

Governor Ted Strickland: "We established one of the ten most aggressive renewable energy standards in the nation."

Political capital and resources are routinely spent on issues that, while important, are not the top challenges facing Ohio and its citizens. Conversely, not enough resources are spent on the problems that hinder Ohio's economic competitiveness. And too often there is the knee-jerk acceptance of stale ideas that simply don't work.

On the right, conservatives believe that taxes should be as low as possible so government has just the resources sufficient to meet its obligations to citizens. This belief arises from the principal that the fruits of a man's labor are his to use as he deems best and that his use is usually more efficient than the government's use. When taxes get too high, the agreed upon obligation to fund necessary government services becomes a confiscatory action where the burden of government is placed unfairly on citizens.

Conservatives also believe that government should be as efficient and effective as possible with the generous tax revenues it receives. Few would argue that government operates as efficiently and effectively as it should. From gold-plated compensation policies to outdated operational approaches, to non-existent productivity measures, to duplicative and wasteful programs, government is truly the last bastion of the costly blue social model discussed in the Chapter 1.

Though I fully understand why Americans for Tax Reform (ATR) provided conservatives who signed its pledge not to raise taxes an out by taking the position that a $1 tax hike offset by a $1 tax cut was okay, this "net neutral" position guts two core beliefs of the conservative movement: namely, that taxes and government spending are too high. A "good" conservative can now keep taxes at a high level to maintain high government spending and obtain the ATR seal of approval. As noted below, this action is deeply problematic.

In Ohio, the list of issues and actions taken by politicians that focus on the wrong problems is long. Many of these are issues and actions that result in less than stellar results and expend finite resources that could be better utilized.

First, for too long, Republicans have adopted a "starve the beast" approach to government. They reduce a specific tax with the belief that it will shrink government. They believe if government doesn't have enough revenue, it will get smaller. In reality, government leaders simply deficit spend at the federal level and find other sources of revenue at the state and local level. Higher fees, lottery proceeds, liquor proceeds, gambling proceeds, privatization, and other "creative" ways are used to bring additional revenue into government.

This starve the beast approach allows government leaders, including Republican politicians, to avoid cutting government spending in any meaningful way. As previously noted, under mostly

Republican rule, Ohio's general revenue fund expenditures have exploded over the last 22 years, exceeding inflation by 2 percent per year on average. The latest two-year budget passed by a Republican legislature and signed by Governor Kasich when facing a projected $8 billion deficit increased general revenue fund expenditures.

With the projected $8 billion deficit and suffering from 21 years of a weak economy compared to other states, I wrote the Buckeye Institute report "Six Principles for Fixing Ohio" in early 2011. The report highlighted six principles that Ohio needed to adopt to get the state out of the economic ditch it was in. These principles were:

- The Past is No Guide for Today's Budget
- Break Labor's Stranglehold: Freedom Absent from Missouri to Maine
- Put Taxpayers and Vulnerable Populations Ahead of Government Pay Scales and Public Sector Unions
- Government Retirements Should Mirror What the Rest of Us Have
- Make Thinking Outside the Box More than a Slogan
- Demand the Federal Government Respect Our Ability to Get Things Done

The first principle focused on the state budget and the sheer growth in spending over the previous two decades. As I wrote in that report:

> In 1990, the general revenue fund expenditures for Ohio stood at just under $11.6 billion. By 2009, it had grown to roughly $27 billion. In just 19 years, Ohio's budget grew by over 131 percent. Even adjusting for inflation, Ohio's budget outpaced inflation by 41 percent. One must ask: What crises occurred during those years to account for such a large increase in government costs? Higher unemployment? Greater poverty? More people who needed more infrastructure?
>
> In 1992, the unemployment rate reached 7.4 percent. By 2000, it had declined to an astonishingly low 4.0 percent. After the dotcom/technology bubble burst in

2000 and the September 11, 2001, terrorist attack, Ohio's unemployment rate climbed back to 6.2 percent in 2003, but declined over the next few years when it hit 5.4 percent in 2006. It stood at 6.6 percent in 2008. With such low unemployment, government growth was not tied to helping millions of out-of-work Ohioans.

In 1993, the poverty rate in Ohio was 13.7 percent. Throughout the 1990s, the poverty rate declined until it hit a low of 9.8 percent in 2000. It remained low over the next four years and then inched back up to 13.3 percent by 2008. As with the unemployment rate, Ohio's budget increases were not due to an exploding level of poverty.

In 1990, the U.S. Census Bureau estimated that Ohio was home to 10,847,115 people. Over the next 18 years, not once did Ohio's population increase by more than 1.0 percent. In fact, the yearly average population growth in Ohio from 1990 to 2008 was 0.3 percent. From 1990 to 2008, Ohio's population increased just 6.3 percent. The growth of government was not driven by a large increase in people who needed more roads, schools, and other government-funded services....

Ohio's spending increased for one simple reason: A strong national economy drove higher revenues into government. Thus, politicians grew government to use those revenues. The fact is that, rather than budget according to real needs or lean revenue forecasts, politicians created budgets based on boom economies.

It is high time Ohio politicians realigned state government spending to a level commensurate with population growth and inflation.

In March 2012, Governor Kasich proposed a $95 million state spending cut, which is just three-tenths of 1 percent of the general revenue fund expenditure budget, and a reduction in state income taxes "paid" for by an increase in taxes on the oil and gas industry in Ohio. Again, I support lower taxes, and on a positive note, Governor

Kasich's tax plan does not appear to increase taxes on Ohioans, which is a good thing for Ohioans. On closer examination, however, Governor Kasich's tax plan reveals fundamental flaws.

First, it continues to ignore the elephant in the room: government spending. The real problem in Ohio (and America) is that government spending has outpaced inflation and economic growth. Shifting tax burdens from individuals to the companies they work for may change the color of the revenue brought into government, but it utterly fails to tackle the spending side of the ledger.

Governor Kasich's tax plan confirms that he accepts the status quo size of state government. Otherwise, he would reduce government to pay for the income tax cut. Remember, Governor Kasich's first budget actually increased general revenue fund expenditures. From 1990 to 2013, Ohio's general revenue fund expenditures will have exploded by 148 percent with a lot of unjustified government growth.

His view that Ohio's "disproportionately low" tax on the energy industry presents him with a windfall opportunity to increase taxes is, frankly, odd for a conservative. Ohio's severance tax on oil is roughly 0.25 percent. Governor Kasich's tax hike proposal would increase the tax sixteen fold to 4 percent. Ohio for once has a competitive tax advantage over other states, thereby making it more attractive for energy industry growth. According to a 2011 study by Kleinhenz & Associates, without any changes, Utica Shale activity will provide an estimated $1 billion in additional windfall taxes and create roughly 200,000 new jobs. Most governors seeking to increase their states' competitiveness for an industry move to lower tax burdens, not increase them.

No matter the political spin, raising taxes on the energy industry will have a negative impact on Ohio's competitiveness and job creation. When politicians in Arkansas raised the severance tax to grab more tax revenue, the energy industry dramatically ramped down operations by approximately 50 percent. The Kasich Administration blames the low price of natural gas for Arkansas' post-severance tax hike decline, but activity in Pennsylvania, which does not have a severance tax, remained high despite the drop in natural gas prices. Business leaders in all industries are very nervous about politicians with "windfall" mentalities. They know "fairness" for one industry today could hit their industries tomorrow, as feeding government spending is what matters.

A third flaw is that Governor Kasich's tax plan contains no real reform and, therefore, represents nibbling on the margins of our problems. Shifting taxes around doesn't lower Ohio's overall tax burden. No matter which group's ranking you use, Ohio's state income tax is in the middle of the pack. That means that Ohio, compared to most other states, isn't a high state income tax location.

Those same rankings place Ohio's local tax burden among the highest in America. Because of Governor Kasich's cuts to local governments, which did not fund a tax cut, local governments, as evidenced by the hundreds of new tax increases passed in the last year, have raised taxes across Ohio. As a result, net taxes on Ohioans have gone up under Governor Kasich making Ohio even less competitive.

Ohioans need major tax reform that lowers the overall state and local tax burden and ratchets down government spending. Failure to do both will drive more entrepreneurs and jobs out of Ohio.

Governor Kasich and his team have used divisive rhetoric to sell the energy tax hike that nearly mirrored language used by President

Obama to push his tax increases. A document titled, "Income Tax Cut – Key Points" produced by the Kasich Administration, states:

> **Who deserves low taxes: Ohioans or out-of-state oil companies?** The question isn't whether or not there will be low taxes. We have low taxes right now, but they only benefit the *out-of-state* oil companies that ship those benefits *out-of-state* to their *out-of-state* investors and shareholders. It's better for *Ohio* if those benefits remain in *Ohio* to benefit *Ohioans*, who will spend that money in *Ohio* and help rev-up *Ohio's* economy.

This rebuke of out-of-state companies and shareholders is unnecessary. After all, we want those companies and individuals to invest more in Ohio. Plus, many of those shareholders are Ohioans, including Ohio's government pension funds.

At the same time Governor Kasich introduced his energy tax hike, President Obama called on Congress to eliminate tax breaks for oil companies noting "You can either stand with the oil companies, or you can stand up for the American people." In response, Republican Senate Minority Leader Mitch McConnell remarked, "If someone in the administration can show me that raising taxes on American energy production will lower gas prices and create jobs, then I will gladly discuss it. Nobody can and the president doesn't."

The *Blade* reported in "Kasich defends plan to slash income tax" that Governor Kasich stated: "We have an opportunity to move the cost on somebody else so we can lower our taxes." To gain support for his tax plan, Governor Kasich, like President Obama, has engaged is pitting one group (other business industries) against another group (the energy industry).

Specifically, according to attendees, the Kasich Administration conducted meetings with various business group leaders and chambers of commerce making the pitch that they should support the tax on energy companies because it will result in a small income tax cut for their business members. Governor Kasich's goal to make energy companies pay for income tax cuts is similar to President Obama's push for the "rich" to pay higher taxes. To put the unfairness of the severance tax hike in perspective, the commercial activity tax paid by all Ohio businesses generates roughly $1.3 billion in tax revenues per year. The Kasich Administration expects the severance tax hike to generate roughly $300 million per year. That means one industry in Ohio, in addition to paying the commercial activity tax, will be forced to pay one-quarter of the total amount paid by all businesses so Governor Kasich can fund a tax cut in his reelection year.

[JINO Alert #2: Media outlets should get the records on who the Kasich Administration met with to discuss the severance tax proposal, as well as the emails of top political appointees (both government email accounts and private email accounts used to evade open records laws) that discussed the severance tax proposal.]

Governor Kasich also commented that he wants to spread the benefits of the Utica Shale discovery to all parts of Ohio. Governor Kasich's views echo President Obama's famous comment on the campaign trail to Toledo's "Joe the Plumber" that he wanted to tax certain Americans to "spread the wealth around."

On June 5, 2012, Andrew Moylan, Vice President of Government Affairs for the National Taxpayers Union, America's oldest grassroots tax group, issued an Open Letter opposing Governor Kasich's severance tax hike. In the statement, Mr. Moylan states:

> Unfortunately, the proposal you have crafted would cancel out many positive effects of an income tax reduction by enacting harsh tax hikes on the oil and natural gas industry. By singling out Ohio energy production for higher taxes, your plan imperils development of a key sector of the economy that could provide thousands of new jobs and a windfall in state tax receipts.
>
> Increasing severance taxes on specific types of wells will limit growth in a largely prospective industry. According to a September 2011 economic impact study by Kleinhenz Associates, development of the Utica Shale using existing tax structures will create a financial boon for Ohio. The study estimates new developments will generate over 200,000 jobs in the state, increasing output by over $22 billion and taxable wages by over $12 billion. Furthermore, each well drilled will generate state and local income taxes, as well as proceeds from a commercial activity tax and the existing severance tax. The proposal to hike the severance tax four-fold on hydraulically fractured wells jeopardizes much of these potential benefits.
>
> There is a better, more fiscally responsible way to achieve income tax cuts: trimming back wasteful spending to reduce the burden of government.

By joining Ohio's small business energy entrepreneurs and other fiscally conservative leaders in Ohio, NTU is promoting the American Dream of Ohioans across our Appalachian counties who cannot afford a sixteen-fold increase of their tax burden as the potential of the Utica Shale formation is just being tapped.

In fact, the early results from the initial wells are substantially less than the projections used by the Kasich Administration to sell its tax hike. Specifically, the Kasich Administration projected that gross revenue per well would surpass $70 million and well costs would be around $5 million. The actual results from the initial wells indicate gross revenues below $20 million and well costs of roughly $10 million. If these results become the average, then the Kasich Administration average tax cut will shrink substantially to below $15 per taxpayer.

By defending job creators from a "spread the wealth" tax hike and helping them keep what they earn, Ohio's energy entrepreneurs will be able to grow their companies by adding jobs and strengthening their communities. By ensuring that our entrepreneurial sprinters run this vital race without being weighed down by unnecessary taxes, those Ohioans will be able to attract more investments here instead of chasing those investments to Pennsylvania, Texas, Oklahoma, North Dakota, or Louisiana.

Governor Kasich likes to resort to a gimmick involving two dimes to show that Ohio's small business energy entrepreneurs don't pay enough in taxes. Ohio's small business energy entrepreneurs get to keep roughly 7 percent of what they earn after taxes. Ohio's current severance tax on oil already takes 0.25 percent, an amount by the way roughly equal to the 0.26 percent commercial activity tax paid by Ohio businesses. Those small business energy entrepreneurs also pay the commercial activity tax so are getting hit twice. If Governor Kasich succeeds in getting his tax hike through Ohio's legislature, Ohio will take a huge share of the net earnings of Ohio's small energy companies, thereby cutting the 7 percent after tax profit margin down to just 4 percent. That type of tax burden will crush some of these companies and cause others to retrench by cutting jobs and investments. With the global economic slowdown, natural gas glut, and declining oil prices, as well as the uncertain job market in Ohio,

Ohio shouldn't kill the rebirth of its energy industry before it even has a chance to compete.

A little over 100 years ago Ohio led the world in energy production. It can do it again if the Obama and Kasich Administrations would just let our energy entrepreneurs do what they do best instead of seeking to impose higher taxes on them.

Why should you care about the severance tax? Because yesterday it was ignoring the Ohio Constitution to grab more casinos taxes and taking funds from local governments to feed government spending; today it is higher taxes on Ohio's energy industry to maintain spending levels; rest assured tomorrow it will be another industry that can afford to pay more to keep government spending high. If Governor Kasich wants to cut Ohio's state income tax for his reelection year, then he should cut Ohio's grossly out of control general revenue fund expenditures that have outstripped inflation by 2 percent on average every year from 1990 through 2013. Governor Kasich should be fighting for a net reduction in taxes for ALL Ohioans, not unfairly picking tax winners and losers among Ohioans.

Unfortunately, some conservative groups like ATR have given cover to Governor Kasich because the net impact of his tax plan is not a net tax hike. Maintaining high taxes should never be applauded. If conservatives now define victory as net zero tax reduction, then our movement is intellectually dead. We can do better than merely tread water.

Tax policies are important, but a bigger influence on economic growth is the existence of workplace freedom laws. As I noted in the "Six Principles for Fixing Ohio" report:

> Of course, tax and regulatory burdens also impact a state's economy. Although many of the forced

unionization states have heavy tax burdens and many of the workplace freedom states have light tax burdens, some heavily taxed workplace freedom states (Idaho, Nevada, and Utah) had the strongest sustained job growth from 1990 to today. Similarly, a few moderately taxed forced unionization states still had weak job growth (Indiana, Illinois, and Missouri). The combination of both a heavy tax burden and forced unionization is deadly when it comes to job growth, as 11 of the 15 worst performing states are ranked in the top 20 for high tax burdens.

Without a doubt, we should aim to lower the tax burden on Ohioans, but shifting the tax burden is not lowering the tax burden. Plus, it falsely promotes the idea that lower state income taxes alone will lead to stronger job growth.

Conservatives who provide cover to politicians who fail to tackle spending are only deluding themselves that government will shrink. Consider this fact: with total control over state government, the biennial budget passed by the Republican General Assembly and signed by Governor Kasich grew state general revenue expenditures more than the previous two year budget signed by a Democratic governor and passed by a Democratic controlled Ohio House.

Yes, I understand the Medicaid flip that occurred, but every governor can select and highlight approaches to justify why the budget is as it is. We taxpayers only can compare the bottom lines. Governor Kasich even had a built-in excuse of a projected $8 billion deficit to show with his first budget that he "got" the spending problem issue. He failed this test.

In April 2011, I recall discussing my budget critique with his team on the 30th floor of the Vern Riffe building. I asked them a simple question: "When do Ohioans see a budget chart that shows general revenue fund expenditures cut to a new baseline as compared to the current trend with parallel dotted lines going off into the future and then a nice shaded area indicating the permanent savings for taxpayers?" They had no response to that basic question, thereby implicitly indicating agreement with Democrats and left-wing think tanks that Ohio government spending is not out of line, or at least not worth fighting to cut.

Streamlining government initiatives is another great sounding campaign promise too many politicians launch with little to no real savings to show. That isn't to say that looking for ways to streamline government isn't an important component of any reform effort. It is. The issue is when political leaders push streamlining as the main avenue by which they will achieve significant savings. For example, it was recently reported that a new $77 million computer system for Medicare was going to help save taxpayers some of the $60 billion per year in Medicare fraud. The computer system, however, hasn't lived up to expectations and only saved taxpayers $7,591 in the first six months of operation.

Frankly, Ohioans would be far better served if legislators and the governor spent less time on the two-year budget—how much really changes from budget to budget?—and more time on digging deeply into programs to determine efficiency and effectiveness.

During Governor Strickland's term, his near undivided focus on green energy as the panacea for Ohio's economic woes generated few jobs but wasted lots of resources. By placing all of Ohio's eggs in the green energy basket, Governor Strickland failed to defend Ohio's natural resources advantage and to take needed action on many other fronts far more critical to turning around Ohio's economy. His adoption of the environmentalist agenda, like President Obama, ignored the power of the market to override those government investments.

As companies discovered an increasing number of new oil and natural gas deposits and methods to extract more deposits from existing wells, the price of subsidized green energy became even less competitive in America and Europe. By imposing regulatory requirements on energy producers to include an increasing amount of expensive green energy in their portfolios, combined with the U.S. Environmental Protection Agency's (EPA) attack on coal-powered plants, Governor Strickland weakened Ohio's natural advantage in energy of rich coal deposits. These moves only resulted in higher energy prices for Ohio consumers and companies.

Roughly 86 percent of Ohio's energy comes from coal-fired power plants. In addition to taking on the EPA more aggressively to defend Ohio's coal advantage and responsibly harness resources in the Utica Shale formation, Ohio needs to push forward in the development of next-generation nuclear energy plants. Ohio also needs to eliminate the renewable energy requirement forcing utility companies to use inefficient and costly alternative energy sources.

Governors Taft and Kasich were not and are not immune from this approach to governing where too many eggs are placed in one basket. Under Governor Taft, Ohio launched the Third Frontier program that provides funds for technology innovation "to create new…products, companies, industries and jobs." A substantial amount of Third Frontier funds have been given to Ohio colleges and universities for research and development programs.

As highlighted in Chapter Two in "The Sources of Economic

Growth in the OECD Countries" by the Organization for Economic Co-Operation and Development, government-funded research and development can "crowd[] out resources that could be alternatively used by the private sector, including private R&D" (pages 85-86). The report noted that, unlike private sector research and development that is "more directly targeted towards innovation and implementation of new innovation processes," government-funded programs "may not raise technology levels significantly in the short run, but they may generate basic knowledge with possible 'technology spillovers.'" The report, however, cautioned against government-led investments because "the latter are difficult to identify, not least because of the long lags involved and the possible interactions with human capital and associated institutions" (i.e., bureaucrats and bureaucracy).

In Governor Kasich's case, JobsOhio clearly represents his main vehicle to revitalize Ohio. Instead of tackling the real issue holding Ohio back—the power and control of private sector labor unions—Governor Kasich spends vast amounts of time promoting JobsOhio. Perhaps in a decade his belief in the ability of government bureaucrats to pick winners and losers in the marketplace will prove well-founded, but the track record of such attempts federally (i.e., Solyndra), in Ohio, and elsewhere is weak, at best.

The early results aren't impressive. Other than spending funds to keep a few headquarters in Ohio that may not have seriously considered leaving, Ohio has lost a few key companies, with Chiquita Brands being the most high profile. Ohio also doesn't appear to be in the running for any major new facilities except a Chesapeake Energy processing plant that may be built—the company is facing severe financial problems—because of the Utica Shale gas discovery not because of JobsOhio or the Third Frontier programs. Of course, Ohio gets expansion opportunities from companies like Honda and Timken who continue to invest in their facilities here, but those companies would face enormous exit costs to relocate operations outside of Ohio.

JobsOhio type programs also encourage corporate rent seekers to take the money offered and do what they had planned to do anyway. For example, one Ohio company CEO told me that he had applied for funds based on adding a certain number of jobs. He indicated that the company was going to add the jobs anyway because the demands of customers required expanding the business. He viewed the free government money as a cost-free opportunity to improve his profitability. As he said, "If the state of Ohio wants to give me money to do what I am going to do anyway, then why not take it?" This company's increase in employees will be used by Governor Kasich to "prove" his approach to economic development is working, but all it proves is that companies know how to get government to subsidize their plans.

Compare that to South Carolina. That state announced at least four new billion dollar manufacturing facilities bringing thousands of high-paying jobs by Bridgestone Tire, Continental Tire, Michelin, and Otis Elevator (from Mexico no less). Shortly after passing a workplace freedom law, Indiana announced the relocation of a manufacturing plant from Illinois and a new manufacturing facility, both by Caterpillar. Ohio never seems to be in the competition for these new big job projects.

Instead of trying to create a quasi-government private equity component in Ohio or using economic development slush funds to pay companies to stay, politicians should focus on creating a robust economic environment conducive to private sector entrepreneurs, investors, and the private sector. If Ohio wants to add jobs, it should free its workers and its companies from the inflated compensation packages of labor unions and the more problematic workplace inflexibility that comes with labor unions.

On taxes, politicians focus all of their attention on cutting the state income tax (which I agree is good), but largely ignore the ever-increasing tax load of local governments in Ohio. Governor Kasich's recent plan to hike taxes on the energy industry to cut income taxes illustrates this issue perfectly. This tax trading just rearranges the deck chairs on the Titanic, as consumers and companies end up paying for the tax hikes. For many Ohioans, their local government tax burdens (property and city income) are larger than their state income tax burdens, so any minimal state income tax reduction gets offset by local property and income tax increases.

In Ohio, a large portion of K-12 funding traditionally has come from the state budget. In his first budget, Governor Kasich significantly cut the funding going to school districts to close the projected deficit. With little ability or political will to realign budgets to reflect these cuts, it was predictable that school districts would push for property tax increases. Ohioans didn't receive any state income tax relief and are getting hit with higher local taxes, resulting in a higher net tax burden.

As I noted in my March 17, 2011, analysis of Governor Kasich's proposed 2012-2013 budget:

> We also find the steep cuts to local governments troubling since Ohio has recently made progress on the tax front. [According to the Tax Foundation] Ohio currently has the 18th highest state and local tax burden (from 7th highest a year earlier). Because of this total tax

burden, we had encouraged Governor Kasich to hold a tax reform summit with representatives from local governments to come up with a solution to Ohio's tax burden. Our belief is that eliminating a tax "here" that pops up again over "there" simply rearranges the chairs on the deck of the Titanic. We need a thoughtful discussion on how to restructure our governmental units and taxes in Ohio to make us competitive with other states.

Instead, Governor Kasich's budget makes deep cuts in funding to local governments and keeps revenues projected to go to local governments. Because of a few solid reforms in procurements and other areas, as well as the projected savings from passage of Senate Bill 5, Governor Kasich's budget presumes that local governments will have the flexibility to adjust their budgets accordingly.

We are not as hopeful. Of note, it does not appear that Governor Kasich's budget makes across-the-board cuts in state compensation packages. As our *The Grand Bargain is Dead: The Compensation of State Government Workers Far Exceeds Their Private-Sector Neighbors* and *Dipped in Gold: Upper-Management Police and Fire Retirees become Public-Service Millionaires* reports demonstrate, government workers in Ohio have compensation packages far beyond what their private sector neighbors have. Governor Kasich should have used the budget to realign state worker compensation packages to the private sector and the new economic normal in Ohio.

If he did not make those tough choices, why does he think local governments will? The reality is that many local government units will look to increase their taxes to replace the lost funding and revenue. As noted in our *Appendix to "Six Principles for Fixing Ohio": School District Charts*, even before these cuts, the 613 school districts were projecting an aggregate deficit of $7.6 billion by 2015 with compensation package costs swallowing 96 percent of projected revenue.

With compensation package costs absorbing so much of local government budgets, the only options local governments will have are (1) get the unions to agree to across-the-board cuts to realign expenses to revenues, (2) cut less senior employees and "unnecessary" programs, (3) increase taxes, or (4) a combination of these options...

Because of the state budget maneuvers, local governments will blame Governor Kasich for the loss of funding and resort to emotional blackmail (i.e., large class sizes, no extracurricular activities, reduced public safety, etc.) to pass tax hikes. Some will fail and some will succeed. Keep in mind that Governor Kasich's budget did not cut taxes in an amount equal to the amount taken from local governments. As a result, our profound concern is that the net impact of his budget on Ohio will be an increase in Ohio's state and local tax burden. Should this concern materialize, Ohio's tax ranking will again rank among the worst, thereby undermining any private sector recovery.

With the crushing defeat of Senate Bill 5, local governments, even if they had the political will to make cuts—cuts Governor Kasich did not ask state workers to accept, are stuck with compensation package costs in existing collective bargaining agreements.

As predicted, with 78 percent of new levies defeated in November 2011, school districts have resorted to the emotional blackmail threats versus asking employees to accept across the board compensation package reductions. As fully discussed in Chapter 7, it is only a matter of time before 50 percent plus one additional voter approve the new levies, thereby leaving a large number of Ohioans with net higher tax burdens. The passage of 57 percent of local levy hikes in March 2012 is proof of this reality.

Another focus is on the use of tax dollars to build infrastructure.

Billions of Ohio tax dollars have been spent on building new facilities for higher education, roads and bridges, sports facilities, solar and wind turbines, parks, government buildings, and even an attempted railroad from Cincinnati to Cleveland. Because of expensive project labor agreements and prevailing wage requirements, many of these infrastructure assets cost substantially more to build than those items should have cost. In Cincinnati's case, taxpayers built palatial new facilities for the Bengals and Reds in a deal that is bankrupting Hamilton County.

During this mad rush over the last four decades, it apparently never occurred to any governor to identify infrastructure that would be needed today to keep Ohio competitive. One glaring example illustrates yet another failure by Ohio's governors.

Ohio is the seventh largest state in America with over 11.5 million people. Ohio has six large commercial airports to provide its citizens and companies air travel options. According to the U.S. Department of Transportation, from busiest to slowest as measured by passenger departure volume, these airports are Cleveland (41st), Cincinnati (51st), Columbus (52nd), Dayton, (78th), Akron-Canton (95th), and Toledo (240th). The metropolitan statistical areas of these seven cities are (with 2010 population and ranking) Cincinnati-Middleton (2,130,151; 27th), Cleveland-Elyria-Mentor (2,077,240; 28th), Columbus (1,836,536; 32nd); Dayton (841,502; 61st); Akron (703,200; 72nd); Toledo (651,429; 81st), and Canton-Massillon (404,422; 128th). The total number of cities that Ohioans can reach via a daily direct flight from those six airports is just 68 cities. There are 343 metropolitan areas in America with populations in excess of 100,000 people.

Talk to any Ohioan who travels for pleasure or any non-Ohioan who comes to Ohio for pleasure and they will tell you how maddening it is given the direct flight limitations. Millions of hours are lost coming to and from Ohio having to make connections in other airports and then getting delayed in those airports due to weather or other technical issues. Other than to San Juan, Puerto Rico; Toronto, Canada; and Paris, France, Ohioans must take a connection flight to another U.S. airport to travel overseas.

Beyond the inconvenience and lost time incurred by pleasure travelers, this weak infrastructure makes it very difficult and expensive for companies to operate in Ohio. In just the last few years, Ohio lost NCR to Atlanta (and Hartsfield-Jackson Atlanta International Airport; 1st), Chiquita to Charlotte (and Charlotte/Douglas International Airport; 11th), and Aston & Black Custom Clothiers to Fort Lauderdale (and Fort Lauderdale/Hollywood International Airport and Miami International Airport; 23rd and 12th, respectively) because those companies were losing millions of dollars in man-hours on flight connections and flight delays reaching medium and smaller markets. This lack of strong airports crushes Ohio's ability to compete. Because of limited flight options, it isn't unusual for residents in one city to travel to another city's airport to catch a more convenient and/or less expensive flight.

Why didn't Ohio's leaders "see" the need for better air travel support and make the investments in infrastructure to facilitate growth in Columbus? The Columbus airport is now landlocked by highways and buildings. Did someone look at how Rickenbacker could have been expanded to replace commercial service at CMH and continue serving industrial traffic that, when combined, would lure more travel options? That would have been a slightly longer commute for those living north of the city, but it might have been worth it if folks could have reached more cities with direct flights.

With Cincinnati's population growing north and east of the city, getting to the airport is taking longer and longer because it is located in Kentucky. Similarly, with the population in Dayton growing south of the city, getting to the airport located to the north of the city is a haul. Why not build a new airport using the existing structure in Wilmington?

For example, it takes roughly 30 minutes to drive from Centerville to the Dayton airport. It would take roughly the same amount of time to drive to Wilmington. It takes 43 minutes to drive from West Chester to the Cincinnati airport. It would take roughly 50 minutes to drive from West Chester to Wilmington. By closing both the Dayton and Cincinnati airports and building a new airport in Wilmington, those combined growing population areas, along with Springfield, Chillicothe, and the rest of southern Ohio, would feed one airport. This larger population base likely would draw more direct flights. With a closer airport, southern Ohio could attract more private sector companies and investments, especially leisure and hospitality companies interested in leveraging the scenic beauty of that area.

I am not specifically advocating for this project, as the delay in building it might have rendered it too costly. Rather, I am trying to make a point that this project should have been seriously considered. The current configuration of airports makes little sense. Our airports and flight options stink.

I experienced first-hand the impact a new airport has on economic development when I lived in Denver. I arrived in Denver three years after Denver International Airport (DIA) replaced Stapleton Airport. Due to incompetent management and rules that awarded contracts to firms incapable of meeting their obligations, DIA went over budget and its opening was delayed. Nonetheless, over the last fifteen years, DIA has been a powerful engine for Colorado with an estimated $22 billion in annual economic impact. Coloradans drive from as far as Fort Collins (1:20) and Castle Rock (:45), but the convenience is well worth it.

One of the more frustrating approaches taken by government leaders is to nibble on the margins of a problem, but claim their actions represent major reform. The latest example of this nibbling habit surrounds the reforms needed to fix Ohio's five government pensions.

As highlighted in the Buckeye Institute report "Hanging by a Thread," Ohio's five government pension plans currently face a $66 billion (and growing) deficit. This deficit is even larger if government pensions have to manage their books using the same rules that private sector pensions are required by law to use. Instead of reforming the five government pensions to permanently reduce the deficit and eliminate the future threat of a bailout being thrust onto taxpayers, the Ohio Senate adopted the meager reforms being proposed by the five government pensions.

These reforms tweak the existing structure by pushing back the allowable retirement age by a few years and by using the highest five years of pay versus the highest three years of pay to calculate pensions. Because Republicans took back the Ohio House and the Governor's Office in November 2010, the government pension plans deleted their plan to have taxpayers pay an even greater share into the pensions.

It is clear there is no political will in the Ohio General Assembly or the Governor's Office to move all new workers into a defined contribution plan (like Michigan did fifteen years ago—again, Ohio the laggard) or to move current workers to a true hybrid plan that matches what private sector Ohioans receive under Social Security and 401(k) plans (what Democratic-led Rhode Island did in 2011). The amount of resources spent on enacting nibbling reforms of a major fiscal problem in Ohio is stupefying.

Finally, Ohio's governors all toe the line when it comes to the federal government. Instead of launching a national debate on the roles and responsibilities between the federal government and state and local governments, Ohio's governors adopt a "Mother May I?" attitude to the federal government. This submissive approach involves acquiescing to federal authority over a host of issues and seeking permission via waivers to deviate from federal mandates.

Beyond the constitutional issues involved with ceding historically state and local authority to the federal government, Ohioans end up subsidizing programs in other states. Using the bully pulpit of the Governor's Office, Ohioans would be far better served fighting back against the continued encroachment of the federal government on issues like education, transportation, Medicaid, and welfare.

For those interested, I will more fully discuss this critical issue in a groundbreaking Heritage Foundation report on competitive federalism coming out later in 2012 available at www.heritage.org/about/staff/m/matt-mayer. If we want to fix Ohio and America, we must focus on the big problems and find permanent solutions. We also must deal with the hurdles placed in our way by state and local reporters who control the content seen by many Ohioans.

4

JINOs (JOURNALISTS IN NAME ONLY)

"0-66."

The liberal bias of the national media is well-known and well-established. In stark contrast, the liberal bias of the media that covers state and local politics is largely unknown and unexplored. This chapter details the very real and damaging liberal bias held by state and local media, at least in Ohio.

If a Tree Falls in the Forest and No One Is There to Hear It...

I have been actively involved in politics for over a decade in three different locations: Colorado, Washington, D.C., and Ohio. When many of my colleagues blamed poor media coverage on liberal media bias, I always insisted that journalists have a financial stake in covering both sides of the debate and, more importantly, a professional duty to uphold their journalistic integrity. From Lynn Bartels at the *Rocky Mountain News* and Julia Martinez at the *Denver Post* who covered two of the top political races in the country of which I was involved to Eric Lipton at *The New York Times* and Lara Jakes at the *Associated*

Press who covered the new homeland security enterprise erected after September 11, 2001, in which I played a role, journalists have treated my side fairly.

Notwithstanding my experience at the national level, many groups have done studies showing the liberal media bias against conservatives. To my knowledge, few studies exist focusing on the liberal bias pervasive in state and local media coverage. Had I not spent a significant amount of time in the trenches, I would have been largely oblivious to that slanted coverage.

Unfortunately, unlike my experience in Colorado, the journalists in Ohio, especially the news reporters from the six big newspapers (*Akron Beacon Journal, Cincinnati Enquirer, Cleveland Plain Dealer, Columbus Dispatch, Dayton Daily News,* and *Toledo Blade*), exhibited a liberal bias against conservative positions. Additionally, week after week taxpayers are short-changed by suburban journalists, as their coverage is grossly one-sided to benefit higher taxes and the entrenched interests. Frankly, many of the people working at those entities aren't journalists in the grand tradition: rather, they are "journalist in name only", or JINOs.

These JINOs give the impression that they present both sides of the story, and you'll find conservatives quoted in many stories. Conservative quotes, however, typically appear at the very end of the story. Many readers never make to the end of most stories and thus miss the other side of the story. This end of the story treatment is used only to provide a thin veneer of presenting "both sides." Naturally, these stories were selected by the JINOs based on their priorities and not on the work done by conservative groups like the Buckeye Institute.

Under my leadership, the Buckeye Institute released ten major reports (and countless smaller pieces) on the big challenges facing Ohio. These reports covered collective bargaining, criminal justice, Medicaid, government pensions, government consolidation, jobs and the economy, and property taxes. As detailed below, these reports significantly influenced policy makers in Ohio.

We also undertook a major redesign of the Buckeye Institute website that resulted in over 6,000,000 searches of government salary data in just 18 months. We created several first-in-the-nation tools for taxpayers to use to educate themselves on their total tax burdens (the Tax Calculator tool), on compensation differences between the public and private sectors (the Job Comparison tool), and the gold-plated nature of government pensions compared to their own retirement plans (the Retirement Comparison tool). Over 1,000,000 visitors have used these innovative tools. As an independent validation of this innovation, the American Institute of Certified Public Accountants is using the Tax Calculator as the model to replicate in the other 49 states.

We even commissioned a groundbreaking poll on the big issues in July 2010. The poll, conducted by Magellan Data and Mapping Strategies on July 19, 2010, surveyed 1,800 registered voters in Ohio. Because of the large sample, the poll's margin of error was only 2.31 percent. The poll asked Ohioans how they would solve Ohio's estimated $8 billion deficit and provided these three choices: reduce government compensation packages, cut government services, or increase taxes. Fifty percent chose reducing government compensation packages and only 16 percent selected higher taxes. More interestingly, 85 percent of Ohioans, including Democrats and labor union members supported giving workers the freedom to choose whether to join labor unions. The top-line results, cross-tabs, and polling presentation were all provided to the media.

Yet, other than two stories on the release of government salary data on the website by Laura Bischoff in the *Daily News*, not one other journalist covered <u>any</u> of the major reports we did, our website innovations, or the stunning poll. If you count each report and the poll and each outlet as an "at bat," we went 0-66 for the game. It is impossible to ignore liberal media bias in the newsrooms after such a statistically shocking outcome.

Interestingly, like Ohioans who showed great interest in our work and website, the editorial side of the newspapers found our work highly relevant by citing the Buckeye Institute more than 20 times during my tenure. Moreover, actual events showed just how relevant our work was. Here are just three examples.

First, three weeks before anyone had heard of Bell, California, and its government compensation scandal, the July 2010 "The Grand Bargain" report highlighted the gross imbalance in compensation between Ohio state government workers and their private sector neighbors. "The Grand Bargain" report laid the intellectual and data foundations for the collective bargaining reforms contained in Senate Bill 5, as well as upcoming pension reforms.

Plus, with over 1,000,000 visitors from 553 Ohio cities doing over 7,000,000 searches of the various government salary tools, the idea that Ohioans don't find government compensation information relevant is laughable on its face. In two separate editorials ("See for Yourself" on September 7, 2011, and "State Issue 2" on October 17, 2011) the *Dispatch*'s editorial board directed Ohioans to use the Buckeye Institute's salary data tools to get the facts on government compensation costs.

As proof of the importance of "The Grand Bargain" report, a union-funded group out of Washington, D.C., did a report to serve as the counter-weight to our report. Unlike our report, that report received an enormous amount of coverage. Even more troubling, JINOs continually referred to the report as the "Rutgers Study" because the author was a professor at Rutgers University, which falsely gave the report the appearance of being the unbiased work of a top university. The report, along with cookie-cutter versions dropped in other states, was bought and paid for by a union-funded group and had no formal tie to Rutgers University. It would be like calling "The Grand Bargain" report a "Duquesne University" report because the authors work in the Economics Department at that university.

Regardless, the *Youngstown Vindicator* correctly noted in a September 4, 2011 editorial in the lead-up to the vote on Issue 2, "SB 5: It's all about the money," that "[t]here are two important studies that reflect the positions of the two sides. For the proponents, the Buckeye Institute for Public Policy Solutions' 'The Grand Bargain is Dead' has become the rallying cry." This editorial represented the second time an editorial in the *Vindicator* had referred to the importance of "The Grand Bargain" report, the first being the April 3, 2011 editorial "Unions and Dems will be tested" which detailed elements of the report. Even the *Plain Dealer*, in a "PolitiFact" column on February 21, 2011, analyzing a claim made by Governor Kasich on government compensation packages that relied upon "The Grand Bargain" report, had to conclude that Governor Kasich's claim was "True." The *Blade* also mentioned the report in a July 18, 2010 editorial "Voters can't handle truth? Try us" and again in a November 3, 2010 editorial

"Governor Kasich."

An even more glaring omission occurred just three weeks before the election in a front-page story in the *Dispatch*. In a comprehensive thirty-eight paragraph article titled, "Public, private compensation in same ballpark," the reporter commited two glaring mistakes. First, he quoted Aristotle Hutras, the director of the Ohio Retirement Study Council (ORSC), as a neutral source in the battle of studies on the compensation differentials between government and private sector workers in Ohio. I know Aristotle. He is a good guy, but describing him as a neutral player is naïve or disingenuous.

Before retiring at the end of 2011, Aristotle spent the last 22 years at the ORSC and is a proud defender of the compensation system of state government. Prior to joining the ORSC, Aristotle worked closely for Democratic Speaker Riffe in the Ohio House. With his $113,000 salary in 2011, Aristotle's government pension in 2012 is estimated to be at least $74,500, with a lifetime payout of roughly $1.7 million (assuming he lives to age 78). Quoting a 33 year government worker whose pension income alone places him in the top 25 percent of all Ohioans as an unbiased source on whether his compensation is too high is absurd.

Second, the reporter went on to cite three studies that looked at the issue. Despite the widespread editorial coverage of "The Grand Bargain" report and my testimony about it at the Senate Bill 5 hearings, it did not make the list of reports covered by the reporter. Instead, he covered a similar report by Andrew Biggs and Jason Richwine that found that Ohio government workers received compensation packages that were 43 percent more lucrative than their private sector peers as the pro-Senate Bill 5 report and two anti-Senate

Bill 5 reports (the "Rutgers Study" and a University of Wisconsin-Milwaukee report that found government workers' total compensation was less than their private sector peers).

Next, the October 2010 Buckeye Institute report, "Dipped in Gold: Upper-Management Police and Fire Retirees become Public-Service Millionaires," exposed for the first time that the Deferred Retirement Option Plan for Ohio police and fire personnel was creating public service millionaires. The November 2011 report, "Hanging by a Thread," detailed the dire fiscal conditions of the five government pensions. Together, the reports focused on one of the biggest issues requiring legislative action: government pension reform. With the over-the-top and erroneous responses by the government pension plans, it is clear these reports were anything but irrelevant.

Despite the lack of news media, the *Dispatch* editorial board read the "Dipped in Gold" report. In its November 18, 2010 editorial "Drop the secrecy," the *Dispatch* said, "The Buckeye Institute for Public Policy Solutions has raised some important questions about a generous deferred-retirement plan available to police officers and firefighters through the Ohio Police & Fire Pension Fund." Its own reporters missed those important questions. The *Vindicator* referred to the "Hanging by a Thread" report in its December 18, 2011 editorial "Public Pensions in Free Fall."

Finally, in November 2010, we released the Buckeye Institute report "Smart on Crime: With Prison Costs on the Rise, Ohio Needs Better Policies for Protecting the Public." The "Smart on Crime" report focused on criminal justice reforms that looked beyond simply locking up more criminals and offered a menu of alternative solutions that cost less and improved recidivism rates. This report contributed to the passage of legislation six months later that adopted many of our recommendations. As with the other three reports noted above, the *Beacon Journal* mentioned the "Smart on Crime" report in its "Within reach of lame ducks" editorial on December 1, 2010.

If Ohioans read only the news sections of the big six newspapers, they would have never known that the Buckeye Institute issued ten data-driven, highly relevant reports in 2010 and 2011. Given the substantial editorial coverage of our work and the widespread interest of Ohioans in it, one has to ask why JINOs at the big six newspapers failed to cover these reports?

More recently, the Buckeye Institute finally got a hit. On March 28, 2012, it released the report, "Ohio Right-to-Work: How the Economic Freedom of Workers Enhances Prosperity," which focused on the issue of workers having the right to choose whether to join labor unions. The "Ohio Right-to-Work" report received coverage in two (*Dispatch* and *Daily News*) of the big six newspapers. This coverage likely only occurred because (1) Ohioans for Workplace Freedom already had qualified ballot language to make Ohio a workplace freedom state, (2) the union-funded We Are Ohio had announced it would aggressively fight the initiative, and (3) Indiana passed a workplace freedom law in February 2012. The report served as additional fodder on an already contentious issue.

Because of the late release of the report as noted below, opponents were able to co-opt the coverage. Specifically, the lead author, Dr. Richard Vedder, did a similar report for Indiana in January 2011. In an effort to stop Indiana from adopting workplace freedom legislation, the union-funded Economic Policy Institute (EPI) released a report critical of Dr. Vedder's Indiana report on January 3, 2012.

For example, the *Daily News* story cited the EPI report to refute the claims in the "Ohio Right-to-Work" report. Consistent with liberal JINO bias, the *Daily News* story included comments from three different groups criticizing the report, but no additional comments from other proponents of workplace freedom. The story also referred to the Buckeye Institute as "right-leaning," but noted that EPI was "nonpartisan" and provided no qualifying description for Policy Matters Ohio (PMO), another left-wing policy group cited in the story.

In terms of the tardiness of the report, consistent with the philosophy during my tenure to set the debate in Ohio by producing reports on the big issues, I contracted with Dr. Vedder and his team to write the report back in January 2011—a full fourteen months before the report finally became public. The report, completed in May 2011, originally was supposed to be released in July 2011, but was delayed until November 2011. For troubling reasons not worth going into, the report, despite my best efforts, did not get released in July or November. Regardless of the timing of its release and the biased coverage it received, this important report now provides data for proponents of a workplace freedom law.

In total contrast, virtually every "report" released by the left-wing, union-funded groups Innovation Ohio, PMO, and EPI (producer of the "Rutgers study") received substantial media coverage. In some cases, "reports" consisted of two to three page press releases with virtually no supporting data and lots of partisan opinion. In fact, virtually any group not on the right side of the ideological spectrum gets coverage of its reports (e.g., The Pew Center, the Mid-Ohio Regional Planning Commission, The Brookings Institute, the Greater Ohio Policy Center, and The Center for Community Solutions). For example, the *Dispatch* gave a Brookings Institution report front page, below-the-fold treatment on May 20, 2012. A search of any of the six major newspaper websites will show this imbalance of coverage.

Another great example is the first report from Innovation Ohio titled, "Ohio Teachers and Collective Bargaining: An Analysis" that purported to show Ohio teachers had received large pay cuts between 2008 and 2009. Reporters at the *Dispatch, Plain Dealer,* and *Daily News* picked up the story on February 28, 2011. Within 24 hours of its public release, I published "A Short Response to the Innovation Ohio Report" that showed that the Innovation Ohio report was erroneous based on data from the Ohio Department of Education. Needless to say, the reporters who wrote the original story failed to cover my response, thereby leaving readers with a false view on teacher pay in Ohio.

Remember, according to statements made to reporters by former Governor Strickland in December 2010, Innovation Ohio was created specifically to counter the Buckeye Institute and the impact it was having. This policy disagreement provided the media with an excellent opportunity to show these two foes at battle. Of course, that would have undermined the credibility of this new left-wing entity on its first day of business.

I don't begrudge those left-wing groups the coverage they get. My concern is that our work did not get any, let alone equal, coverage. This failure on the part of those entrusted with the responsibility to fairly and accurately provide readers with news important to them puts taxpayers at an enormous disadvantage when it comes to making informed decisions. Chapter 6 shows how this JINO failure impacted the outcome on Senate Bill 5.

The Overlooked Bias of Weekly Newspapers

Even more troubling for taxpayers should be the type of journalism practiced by some suburban newspapers. In suburban weeklies across the state, city managers and school superintendents are given weekly columns to promote their "accomplishments" and write property tax levy campaign propaganda masquerading as official business. Opponents of property tax levies, at best, are limited to writing 400 words or less op-eds or letters to the editor to push back against the weekly assault.

When the "news" stories from JINOs are added to the mix, taxpayers are hard-pressed to find a reason to vote against property tax levies. In the Central Ohio market, the *This Week* suburban newspaper is the case study on such reporting (now known as *This Week Dublin Villager*). *This Week* spends precious space week after week doing nothing more than reporting what the cities and school districts want it to report. Story after story contains not one shred of critical coverage or opposition viewpoints. Let me give you a few examples.

In the fall of 2010, the Washington Township Fire Department in northwest Central Ohio had a property tax levy on the ballot. Over the course of four straight weeks, a JINO wrote four front-page stories about the levy. Here are the stories with approximate word counts and locations on the front page noted:

- "WTFD's jobs extend beyond fires," 434 words, above the fold (October 7, 2010);
- "Fire levy would keep current services," 450 words, below the fold (October 14, 2010);
- "WTFD: Levy will maintain services, purchase equipment," 386 words, above the fold (October 21, 2010); and
- "Fire department asking for levy support," 564 words, below the fold, (October 28, 2010).

These four stories contained over 1,800 words in 66 paragraphs. Not once did the JINO present an opposing view on the property tax levy or ask a critical question. For example, with 70 percent or more of all calls being for non-fire related issues, has the district reanalyzed its staffing and equipment needs? Have employees taken compensation reductions to share the fiscal pain of their neighbors? Week after week the JINO simply wrote pieces on the positives of passing a tax increase.

Here is a second example. In 2011, Dublin City Schools put a property tax levy and bond issue on the ballot that would have been the third tax hike in seven years (2004, 2008, and 2011) equating to a total tax increase on struggling homeowners of more than 70 percent. Again, the JINO's coverage looked more like she worked for Dublin City Schools than the reporting of a truly balanced reporter. In just one edition of *This Week*, the JINO managed to produce three front-page puff pieces on the levy:

- "Osborne: Without levy, deficit likely in 2013," 430 words, above the fold (October 13, 2011);
- "Axner: Expect $7.5M in cuts next fall if levy is rejected," 480 words, above the fold (also on October 13, 2011); and
- "District: Levy is key to maintaining excellence," 549 words, below the fold (also on October 13, 2011).

In a single edition of *This Week*, the JINO spent over 1,450 words presenting readers with an unequivocally one-sided view of the levy. She failed to find a single critic of the levy or report any answers to tough questions from either Superintendent David Axner or Treasurer Stephen Osborne about the levy.

The JINO's failure occurred despite a September 5, 2011 story in the *Dispatch*, *This Week's* parent newspaper, highlighting the fact that Superintendent Axner's compensation package is 39 percent more than the next highest paid superintendent in Central Ohio. I was quoted in that story criticizing highly paid superintendents for failing to lead by example by reducing their compensation packages. Superintendent Axner listed the parade of horribles that will occur in the district if voters reject the levy, but the JINO never reports information on if district-wide base compensation reductions, including for him, were on the table before cutting staff and/or programs or raising taxes again.

After all, personnel costs reflected the single biggest expense in the district. Yet, the district projected those costs to far outstrip inflation and continually go up—25 percent in just five years. This trend indicated a refusal to ask district employees to realign compensation package costs to reflect the already generous tax revenues Dublin residents provided it. In fact, according to the district's October 2010 five-year fiscal projection, in 2011, personnel costs totaled $147,266,993, or 91 percent of all revenue for the year. A five percent total compensation cost reduction would yield the district the $7.5 million it needed to reduce expenses.

Here are several pieces of information the JINO never reported to readers concerning Dublin City Schools:

- It has finished or is projected to finish the school year with a deficit in seven out of eight years from 2008 to 2015, including the years following the passage of the last levy in 2008;
- If the 2011 levy passed, school property taxes on Dublin homes would have gone up roughly 74 percent from 2004 to 2012;
- From 2001 to 2010, as inflation went up 24 percent, per pupil spending went up 51 percent from $8,511 to $12,881;
- From 2000 to 2011, Dublin's per pupil spending increased from the 72nd highest in Ohio to the 37th highest in Ohio;
- From 2001 to 2010, the average teacher salary jumped by 43 percent;
- The district projects personnel costs will swallow 112 percent

of all revenue by 2015 unless a fourth levy is passed by that date;

- Unless the 2011 levy and a fourth levy are passed by 2015, the district will have a structural deficit of over $56 million; and
- That all of these facts existed before the state budget cuts to local schools occurred in the spring of 2011.

No matter your views, voters certainly would have found that information useful as they mulled over the levy-bond request.

[JINO Alert #3: Media outlets should request and report the data on the issues noted above as school districts and other government entities seek additional tax revenues.]

Regardless of the city, few JINOs appear interested in doing any good old fashion investigative reporting. For example, in looking at the absentee data for Ohio's school districts according to the Ohio Department of Education, Dublin City Schools' teachers are absent 6.3 percent of the school year, or 11.58 days per teacher (over 100,000 hours a year). This rate is up 3.5 days per teacher since the 2000-2001 school year. With a median teacher salary of $70,728, Dublin taxpayers are losing over $4.1 million per year in teacher time, as well as the educational value of having those teachers in the classroom. With a $20 per hour required substitute cost, taxpayers also must cover more than $2 million in substitute teacher payments. Because Dublin teachers are contractually limited to 185 days, when the 11.58 absentee days are factored in to the equation and pay is pro rated to the 260-work day schedule of most workers, Dublin teachers make the equivalent of a median salary of $106,000.

Statewide, the Ohio Department of Education data indicates that teachers are absent 9.1 days per school year. The lost time due to absences is over $300 million per year. Assuming a $20 per hour substitute cost, Ohio's school districts are spending nearly $143 million per year to replace absent teachers. This analysis is not intended to say that teachers are not allowed to get sick. They are and, given the germs brought into the classroom by kids, will get sick. Absent time, however, does not cover only when a teacher is sick. It covers when a teacher is out of the classroom. I am merely illustrating data that taxpayers may want to know as they are asked to approve a request for higher taxes.

[JINO Alert #4: Media outlets should get this attendance and substitute cost data and inform readers about it.]

The October 13, 2011 *This Week* looked like one of those annoying television ads for mattresses where pop-ups continually appear to ensure that the viewer has to be utterly brain-dead to not get that a big sale is going on. Specifically, the front page contained two big black and green blocks containing the phrase "A closer look." Under each block, the paper describes an element of the story. For the story focused on Superintendent Axner's comments, the description contained the emotional blackmail school districts use to scare voters into supporting levies. It read:

> Superintendent David Axner said the district would have 25 students in kindergarten and first-grade classes, 27 students in grades 2 and 3, and 30 students in grades 4 and 5. In the middle and high schools, classes would carry a 30-1 student-to-teacher ratio, he said. Other areas facing potential cuts include supplemental contracts, stipends, professional development, field trips, maintenance, reading support, educational options and busing.

Threatening bigger class sizes is the nuclear bomb of failed school district levy campaign cuts, so highlighting this cut would guarantee readers would "get the message."

Not only is this reporting biased against taxpayers, but it also represents indirect financial support of school district levy campaigns. Without such one-sided reporting, levy proponents would have to expend campaign funds to get out their message. Opponents simply cannot compete with such a stacked deck. How are taxpayers expected to make informed decisions given the onslaught of pro-levy media coverage? The reporting failure on the part of JINOs virtually ensures that taxes will go up.

Can't We All Just Get Along

Here is one last example of the problem with Ohio's news coverage. No matter where one turns, media pundits are always lamenting the divisiveness of politics in Ohio and in Washington today. These pundits constantly call for more bipartisanship. They yearn for the good ol' days before term limits when things got done (conveniently ignoring the lack of term limits in Congress and its similar hyper-partisanship) – the days when Governor Rhodes and Speaker Riffe would cut deals to make things happen (or before term limits kicked in when Republicans totally controlled state government). Of course, given Ohio's systemically weak economy and high state and local tax burden, the benefit of getting things done didn't work out so well for taxpayers.

Some quick background.

After appearing on a radio program with John Begala, Executive Director of The Center for Community Solutions, a center-left group focused on health care issues, I reached out to John to start a dialogue because he came across as someone who might be interested in putting aside the sharp elbows and seeing if we could get something done together. John had been an elected Democratic state representative from Cleveland in the 1970s, but his June 2010 report "Thinking the Unthinkable: Finding Common Ground for Resolving Ohio's Fiscal Crisis" had some non-liberal ideas in it.

Over the course of time, John and I came up with tax expenditure reforms that we both could agree on. Tax expenditures are tax benefits such as a tax credit given to a specific group that reduces the tax burden for members of that group. The reforms consisted of three elements: (1) eliminate roughly $300 million in specific tax expenditures, (2) enact a sunset review of all tax expenditures to ensure each expenditure still made sense and require reauthorization after each review, and (3) appoint a nonpartisan committee to review Ohio's state and local tax system and make recommendations to improve it. We asked a third group, the center-left Greater Ohio Policy Center, to join us on seeking legislative support for those reforms.

Our nonpartisan effort received support in many editorials. Specifically, the following editorials from five of the big six newspapers cited our work:

- *Plain Dealer*, "When 3 think tanks with quite different outlooks agree on a list of tax loopholes to close, Ohio's leaders should listen" (May 21, 2011)
- *Beacon Journal*, "Ready for scrutiny" (May 22, 2011)
- *Blade*, "Close tax loopholes" (May 29, 2011)
- *Daily News*, "Tax breaks not free; they put drain on budget" (June 9, 2011)
- *Dispatch*, "Ripe for Review" (June 10, 2011)
- *Dispatch*, "Short Takes" (September 24, 2011)
- *Plain Dealer*, "Cheers & Jeers" (December 1, 2011)

With such near unanimous support from the editorial pages, it became harder for elected officials to ignore this nonpartisan effort, and an effort is currently underway to institute many of our ideas.

In the process of our discussions, we decided to join forces for a big ideas conference that would explore the major issues facing Ohio with top-notch experts from across the political spectrum. We wanted to demonstrate that ideological opponents could sit down and find areas of common ground. Doing so doesn't require putting aside your principles, it just means finding the overlapping part of the Venn diagram (those diagrams with two overlapping circles) where agreement is possible.

On December 8, 2011, we brought in nationally recognized experts from across the United States to speak on government consolidation, health care, government pensions, taxes, and constitutional changes to Ohio's 1851 Constitution. All of these issues are expected to be top agenda items in 2012 and 2013. Over 300 people attended the event just a block from the Statehouse where many reporters and, of course, elected legislators spend their days.

The event included a lunchtime debate between two of the world's top economists, Drs. Alice Rivlin and Arthur Laffer. Dr. Rivlin served as the first director of the Congressional Budget Office, as the Budget Director under Bill Clinton, and as a member of the National Debt Commission. Dr. Laffer is the father of supply-side economics and the Laffer Curve. Both Drs. Rivlin and Laffer have advised many presidents, prime ministers, and other world leaders over the last forty years. Their presence on the same stage anywhere, let alone in Ohio, was unprecedented.

Other than a short blog piece on the *Enquirer* website, the event and, more specifically, the Rivlin-Laffer Debate received no print news media attention. Zero. Zip. Zilch. I do have to give special kudos to the team at WCMH-NBC4 and evening anchor Colleen Marshall, who moderated the debate and spent most of the day at the event, as well as Karen Kasler, Statehouse Bureau Chief of Ohio Public Radio & Television. Not even the *Dispatch*, which sponsored the event, provided coverage of it. Both Ms. Marshall and Ms. Kasler felt the event was important enough to cover. In fact, based on attendance records, other than Ms. Marshall and Ms. Kasler, despite at least six weeks notice, only one reporter and just a handful of legislators even took the time to attend the event. Had Drs. Rivlin and Laffer done this event in New York City, Washington, D.C., Chicago, or Los Angeles, you can guarantee that it would have received significant media coverage.

The only conclusion I can take away from the lack of media coverage of this nationally unique event is that, despite the call for unity, JINOs and Ohio's political pundits find conflict much more newsworthy. In economic terms, if you reward conflict, you'll get more of it. Perhaps JINOs contribute to the political dysfunction in America and in Ohio due to what they choose to cover and not to cover.

Without a doubt, the failure of the local media in Ohio to fairly cover important issues places taxpayers at an enormous disadvantage. It's one of the reasons Ohio's taxpayers don't stand a chance.

5

THE POWER OF ENTRENCHED INTERESTS

Lobbyist: "Term limits is the single worst law in the history of Ohio."

When the Founding Fathers designed our Constitution, they adopted a series of refinements to ensure that the ability of factions to control the government was minimized. These refinements included the separation of powers across the three branches of government, the manner and mode of elections for the President and the Congress, the systems of checks and balances, and the allocation of rights and powers between the federal government and the states.

Because America is a republic, not a direct democracy, the Founding Fathers sought to ensure that the elected federal government represented the various interests outside of Washington. The House of Representatives, being popularly elected by the people, served to protect the interests of the people within their congressional districts, and districts were allotted to states by population totals. The Founding Fathers thought that the small house districts would serve as a check on the ability of local factions to gain control of the levers of the federal government to enact bad laws or oppress opponents.

In contrast to the House of Representatives, the Senate was comprised of two senators from every state who were elected by the state legislatures. The senators' primary role was to represent the interests of their states, which might, at times, be in conflict with the majority of people of the states. The fundamental reason why senators were elected by state legislatures was because that process guaranteed that the senators would fight in Washington for the interests of the states. The equality of representation among the states served as a check so that large states could not exert undue influence over the small states, which could be done in the House due to the allocation of seats by population.

The President was elected in a manner that gave both the people and the states a role in his election, and he served to represent America writ large (both the people in America and the states that form America). Specifically, the people vote for electors in each state who are then certified by the state to support the candidate who receives the most votes in the Electoral College process. This dual representation means that there will be times, rare as they have been, where the majority interest of the states overrides the majority interest of the people in order to further weaken the ability of a faction to control the Presidency.

This brief constitutional history lesson is important because it demonstrates the importance of protecting government from the power of factions, or entrenched interests. At the state and local levels, the adoption of civil service laws served as another attempt to weed out patronage or minimize the ability of entrenched interests to control government. The ever-increasing transparency of campaign contributions, including the financial limitations placed on donors, represents yet another attempt to monitor those seeking to influence government.

Unions Own Ohio

In Ohio and the United States today, there are several categories of entrenched interests ranging from big business to single-issue groups on the left and the right. Whether represented by the pork barrel spending out of Washington, D.C., or the corporate welfare masked as economic development out of state government, big business and its lobbyists certainly do well.

Big business, however, tends to shy away from the big reform issues, as rocking the boat could lead them to lose their spoils or make them a target of labor unions or transparency groups. I recall the time at a meeting of industry players in June 2010 when one top representative of Ohio businesses went into a tirade about the workplace freedom issue and how such an issue was just a right wing distraction. I wonder if he'd say that to Governor Mitch Daniels now that Indiana has enacted workplace freedom legislation and Caterpillar is moving operations to that state.

Another set of rising interest groups are the various independent groups that have been created after the U.S. Supreme Court's decision in *Citizens United v. Federal Election Commission*. The *Citizens United* decision lifted the monetary donation restrictions on corporations and unions to groups that were independent and that did not coordinate with candidates. As the *Financial Times* reported on May 9, 2012, in "Super-Pacs rack up the cash for Republicans' election campaign," groups like Karl Rove's American Crossroads on the right and the pro-Obama group Priorities USA Action on the left will inject nearly $500 million in political ads to the presidential race in 2012. With labor unions already spending hundreds of millions of dollars on political campaigns for Democratic candidates, many supporters see the rise of Super-PACs as a leveling of the playing field for Republicans.

Without a doubt, however, the single most powerful entrenched interest in America today is Big Labor. Unlike big business that spreads its campaign contributions to both political parties based on who controls the levers, labor unions direct almost all funds to the Democratic Party and do so at a level unrivaled over the last few decades.

According to Anthony Davies, an Associate Professor of Economics at Duquesne University:

> From 1989 to 2009 unions donated more money to political candidates than did any other industry or special interest group. Unions donated twice as much to politicians as did all telecommunications, insurance, tobacco, pharmaceutical and real estate firms combined. Spending member dues on a narrow partisan agenda is central to the way today's unions work. While corporations tend to hedge their bets by splitting their donations evenly between Republicans and Democrats, 90% of labor union donations go to Democrats.

In fact, using campaign data from OpenSecrets.org, Davies notes that labor unions have donated more than $500 million to Democrats nationally from 1989 to 2009. The amount is just a fraction of what labor unions spend to influence elections.

Based upon reports from the U.S. Department of Labor, labor unions spent over $2.2 billion on campaign activities such as paid election day workers, phone banks, and campaign commercials over the last two election cycles. Media reports have documented that labor unions spent nearly $500 million in 2008 alone on behalf of President Obama. This financing juggernaut keeps Democrats in line and instills fear into weak-kneed Republicans. Big business and conservative groups simply can't compete with this amount of money.

In Ohio, in their effort to defeat Senate Bill 5, the labor unions and their allies raised $42 million. Labor unions believe they own Ohio. As AFSCME President Gerald McEntee noted in his official statement on June 6, 2012, following the devastating recall election loss in Wisconsin, "We will take them on, just as we did in Ohio, where we overturned John Kasich's anti-collective bargaining bill."

To put that amount in perspective, according to the *Blade*, the total spent in 2010 on the Governor's race by both John Kasich and Ted Strickland totaled $33 million. In Wisconsin, labor unions and their allies have spent over $20 million to repeal the collective bargaining reforms enacted by Governor Walker, including funding a Supreme Court race, recall elections of State Senators, and a repeal effort aimed at Governor Walker. Nationally, labor unions are constantly attempting to cash in on their campaign contributions in support of President Obama by getting him to stack the National Labor Relations Board with union zealots and to attack attempts by companies to grow in states that protect workers' right to choose whether or not to join unions.

In Ohio, as several Republicans in the Ohio House and Senate defected from the party and voted against Senate Bill 5, not one Democrat had the guts to break with the party and the labor unions to vote for Senate Bill 5. Many of the Democrats in the Ohio House and

Senate come from county or city elected positions. They know the fiscal crises hitting local governments, and they know the single biggest driver of those crises is the compensation package costs of local government workers.

Not only did the Democrats vote against Senate Bill 5 *en masse*, but they also failed to offer any amendments in the Ohio House or Senate to moderate the bill. Why? Because the labor unions won't tolerate <u>any</u> reforms to Ohio's pro-union collective bargaining law.

As Democrats in other states buck the labor unions, in Ohio, the only bucks the Democrats appear to care about are the bucks coming from labor unions into their campaign coffers.

Public Sector Collective Bargaining Is Anti-Taxpayer

Labor union power in Ohio results in high taxes for Ohioans and a weak jobs economy. Setting aside the negative economic impact unionization has on the private sector, the impact it has on government is to drive compensation package costs higher, to protect weak or bad employees, and to increase inefficiency in government. We are talking about <u>government</u> employers, not evil corporate CEOs or sweatshop bosses. Do Ohioans really need labor unions to ensure that government employers properly treat government workers? Of course, the answer is no.

Unlike the private sector where management is driven by the profit motive, government managers lack a profit motive, which is a powerful driver of <u>both</u> management and employee behavior. A profit allows management to reward employees, reinvest in operations, and provide returns to investors.

For management and employees, operating a company at a loss

results in either layoffs, the termination of poorly performing individuals or units or, ultimately, the end of the company where all workers lose their jobs. Nowhere is this reality better illustrated than with General Motors and the United Auto Workers (UAW).

Due to inferior products and high labor costs, General Motors first laid-off workers and shut down weak product lines. Even the UAW had to face reality and agree to a two-tiered labor contract where new UAW members receive significantly lower pay than veteran UAW members for the same work. General Motors still required a taxpayer bailout in 2009 to stabilize its operations. Time will tell if this bailout worked.

Other private sector companies, their workers, and, if present, their labor unions routinely face this profit motive. The profit motive serves as a cold splash of water on the face of labor unions and their members who sometimes seem to believe that money grows on a money tree just out back behind the plant. A company can only continue operations for so long without making a profit before it must close it doors.

No similar end-point exists in government. Because government management, government workers, and their labor unions aren't constrained by a profit motive, labor relations tend to be far less contentious. When the economy is doing well enough, tax revenues hide the greater than inflation compensation package increases given by government management to government workers. For example, from 1991 to 2008, state workers in Ohio received annual base increases totaling 53 percent, or 3 percent per year on average, as inflation only increased by 2.8 percent per year on average. You may be thinking, 0.2 percent more isn't that much, is it?

Surplus tax revenues also concealed the extreme perquisites awarded by government management to government workers that drove the average yearly total salary increases of government workers from 3 percent to well beyond 5 percent per year—more than 2 percent per year more than inflation. These perks include longevity pay, step pay, banked sick and personal leave, overly generous overtime policies, pension pick-ups, and gold-plated pensions.

When the major recession hit in the fall of 2008 and tax revenues flowing to state and local governments slowed significantly, government managers were left holding empty bags with which to meet the obligations of benefits they had promised government workers. Unlike General Motors and the UAW, because government can't go out of business, government labor unions largely refuse to agree to base compensation reductions. Instead, they push the problem down the road by freezing one of three pay components (i.e., step increases are frozen, but base salary and longevity increases continue) for a year or two with the hopes that tax revenues increase again and allow the gravy train to continue.

Compounding the problems surrounding the lack of a profit motive in government, labor unions actively work to elect politicians into government management so that they negotiate union contracts with the very same people whom they helped elect. Despite their obligation to represent the interest of taxpayers over the interest of labor unions, many elected officials will place the interest of labor unions and their members ahead of the burden on taxpayers.

The actions by Democrats on Senate Bill 5 highlight this conflict. Despite the fact that without collective bargaining reforms, taxes across Ohio will have to increase in order to cover the compensation package costs of government workers. Not one Democrat in the Ohio House or Senate put taxpayers first and bucked the government labor unions. Even after the veto referendum defeat of Senate Bill 5, not one Democratic legislator has offered even minimal statewide collective bargaining reforms to help local governments deal with the compensation cost issue.

Facing a projected deficit due to its large government compensation costs, Columbus Mayor Michael Coleman and his labor union allies pushed through a city income tax hike. The tax hike allowed him to avoid realigning compensation costs to fit the generous revenues already provided by residents. Not surprisingly, Mayor Coleman opposed Senate Bill 5 and its reforms that would have provided him greater power to control compensation costs.

Mayor Coleman's support for labor unions over residents, however, makes those powers unnecessary. As Jack Reall, head of the firefighter union, commented in a television interview, he doesn't worry about Mayor Coleman, he worries about the boogieman who will be mayor after Mayor Coleman. Shortly before the veto referendum vote on Senate Bill 5, the *Dispatch* revealed evidence of Mayor Coleman's far too cozy relationship with labor unions when it reported unusual contract negotiations occurring in Mayor Coleman's office over a weekend with Mr. Reall. The office usually charged with negotiating labor union contracts for the city was only tangentially involved with the negotiations.

Within the structure of collective bargaining negotiations, the lack of a profit motive for government management allows human nature's abhorrence of interpersonal conflict to drive favorable deals for government workers. Specifically, people hate interpersonal conflict and really hate being placed in the role of the "bad guy" in the workplace, so they concede to generous terms. Some motivating force must override those feelings. In the private sector, because managers must continue to work with the workers who will be impacted by the negotiations, the profit motive serves to override their dislikes of being the bad guys. If labor costs aren't constrained and the company goes belly up, management is out of work, too.

There are two reasons why Ohioans aren't more engaged in fighting the most entrenched and powerful interest. First, due to very good marketing and constant repetition by labor unions, taxpayers still believe that government workers are underpaid and that they engage in public service. The second reason, as covered in Chapter 4, is the lack of media coverage given to opposing arguments such as those put forth in "The Grand Bargain" report and the government salary data and comparison tools on the Buckeye Institute website.

The reality is that government workers are no different than private sector workers. Just as the private sector possesses bad apples, so too does the government. Here are a few recent headlines detailing this fact:

- "Jimmy Dimora federal racketeering trial: Contractor put in cabinets for free around Dimora's pizza oven," February 6, 2012, *Plain Dealer*;
- "Ex-Ohio teacher convicted in student sex case," October 27, 2011, *USA Today*;
- "Ohio State Trooper Arrested for Driving 102 MPH While Drunk," February 18, 2012, *10TV.com*;
- "Columbus school-bus driver held boy and told girl to hit him, police say," March 5, 2012, *Dispatch*;
- "Tutor: 'I've taken to fondling' the students," August 22, 2011, *Dispatch*;
- "Teacher, aide bullied student, 14," November 8, 2011, *Dispatch*; and

- "Cleveland fire inspector accused of taking bribes," June 7, 2010, *Plain Dealer*.

With compensation packages exceeding those packages in the private sector, there is no reason, except for those workers who put their lives on the line to keep us safe, to believe that government work is somehow more noble or sacrificial than private sector work. In fact, given the trust we place in government workers, especially teachers and public safety officers, failures are all that much more devastating.

If taxpayers ever hope to slow the increase in taxes, they must understand that government workers make a lot more than they do for the same type of work and that working in the private sector is as noble as government work. The larger answer is because, beyond being too busy living their lives, the time and money each Ohioan would need to give to fight the labor unions is far greater than the cost they incur due to labor unions, or so they think. This outcome is basic public choice theory.

Specifically, the cost of each labor union contract is spread across lots of people (the bigger the jurisdiction, the more people carry a portion of the cost), so each person "sees" only a small part of the total cost in their taxes. In contrast, the benefit is concentrated among a very small group of government workers who each receive a sizable benefit. Due to this diffusion of the cost and concentration of the benefit outcome, taxpayers don't stand a chance and lose either way. Ohioans naturally don't see the point in engaging in a fight that will cost them more than they will pay under the new labor union contract.

Because of these misunderstandings and cost-benefit hurdles, it is important to engage in a widespread education effort to counter the mythology of government workers and more directly tie those myths to the growing tax burden hitting Ohio taxpayers.

If you doubt that government labor unions are Ohio's most powerful interest, ponder this question: what business interest in Ohio has thrived over the last three decades without any legislation to curb its power or ability to operate? The answer, of course, is none.

Once the Democrats jammed through Ohio's collective bargaining law in 1983, only one piece of legislation amended that law to curb the power of the labor unions. As detailed in the next chapter, the labor unions crushed that effort. In fact, because of the very nature of collective bargaining, government labor unions have increased their power substantially, as government management gave away more and more power and benefits during each round of bargaining. Today, virtually no issue escapes Ohio's mandatory bargaining requirement.

That is pure, unadulterated power, and no entrenched interest uses its power more effectively than labor unions. The next chapter shows what happens when proponents of collective bargaining reforms fail to explain how those reforms are directly related to the ever-increasing tax burden on Ohioans.

6

THE MISSED OPPORTUNITY TO REFORM OHIO'S COLLECTIVE BARGAINING LAW

Governor John Kasich: "We've moved on."

Where to begin?

The table, so the speak, could not have been set better for passing major reform of Ohio's pro-union collective bargaining law. First, Republicans came out of the November 2010 election with control over every statewide office, including the Governor's Office. Republicans increased their control over the Ohio Senate and reclaimed the Ohio House, with an even larger majority than they previously had in 2008. Politically, Republicans could enact the policies that they had heretofore failed to enact from 1993 to 2006.

Next, the issuance of "The Grand Bargain" report in July 2010 highlighted the compensation differential between government workers and their private sector neighbors. The data on pay, health care, sick leave, and pensions showed how good government workers had it. Additionally, the redesigned Buckeye Institute website contained salary data for government workers at all levels of government, including the estimated gold-plated pensions those workers would receive. These two items provided the tools to educate voters on the cost side of the issue.

Entering 2011, state government possessed a projected $8 billion budget deficit. Based on the October 2010 five-year financial projections by the school districts, those entities faced another $7.6 billion deficit by 2015, with compensation costs projected to swallow nearly 100 percent of all revenues. The five government pension plans carried structural deficits of more than $60 billion. When the deficits in Ohio's counties, cities, townships, and villages were added to the mix, Ohioans faced a funding crisis in excess of $80 billion.

On the economic front, Ohio's private sector bled more than 500,000 jobs over the last decade. Ohioans who still had jobs experienced pay cuts, increased health care costs, reduced employer contributions to their retirement plans, and other compensation package cuts.

In the summer of 2011, nearly 50 percent of Ohio counties would issue their triennial property reappraisals that would confirm what many Ohioans feared: they had suffered massive losses in the equity in their homes, with many mortgages now exceeding appraised home values. Finally, no matter which group's ranking you looked at, Ohio possessed one of the highest state and local tax burdens in the country. So, Ohioans faced a fundamental choice: raise taxes to eliminate the deficits while maintaining the gold-plated compensation packages of government workers or realign government compensation packages to reflect the generous tax revenues Ohioans already provide government.

That choice, unfortunately, is not what voters were presented in the fall of 2011.

An Absolute Lack of a Strategy

On January 1, 2011, two key facts should have led Republican leaders to form a detailed and coherent strategy on any plan to reform Ohio's collective bargaining law. After all, Ohio is one of the strongholds of labor unions and any reform would represent a serious threat to their existence and to unions across the country. If Ohio could curb the power of labor unions, any state could.

First, a prior attempt to amend the law made in 1995 by tweaking the definition of "inherent management rights" saw strong labor union and Democratic opposition. The fact that the law had not been altered in 28 years signaled the power of labor unions and, therefore, the need for perfect execution.

Second, Ohio's veto referendum law had been on the books since 1912. The veto referendum process had been used successfully to repeal legislation just three years earlier, namely, to repeal a payday lending law cap in 2008. Given that the Democrats and their labor union allies had no meaningful legislative ability to stop reform legislation, it was all but certain they would use the veto referendum process to overturn whatever legislative reforms were enacted.

These two facts meant that proponents of reform would need to develop a plan that went far beyond the legislative process. They would need to defend the reforms to the voters in a veto referendum election. This required a strategic plan detailing what the message would be, who the messenger(s) would be, how much money needed to be raised, and a strong organizational plan. This plan also needed to spell out how they were going to educate voters throughout the process, win editorial board support, bring in the business community, and loop in local government leaders to support the effort. Apparently, none of this planning occurred.

Senator Shannon Jones introduced Senate Bill 5 on February 8, 2011. This seemed to surprise many Republican leaders. This reaction was the first indication that they did not have a "team" strategy. I knew Senator Jones had been working on legislation for some time, as we had discussed policy options briefly the previous year when we ran into each other at an event.

Governor Kasich had never said a word during his campaign about taking on the issue, so no one knew where he stood on the bill. After winning the November election, he stated that he would do what Governor Mitch Daniels did and reverse an Executive Order issued by Governor Strickland that unionized home health care and child care workers. Unfortunately, no such action was taken in January 2011 or since. In Governor Kasich's defense, he had a two-year budget to develop by mid-March that needed to eliminate an $8 billion deficit without raising taxes.

Unfortunately, shortly before Senator Jones introduced Senate Bill 5, Governor Kasich was recorded at a meeting with employees of the Ohio Environmental Protection Agency referring to a police officer three times as an "idiot." Though the video had been posted on YouTube on January 28, 2011, it did not gain media attention until February 15, 2011, just as the hearings began on Senate Bill 5. Any chance the reform side had at keeping fire and police on the sidelines evaporated as the video gained widespread coverage. Now reform proponents would have the difficult task of countering powerful emotional campaign videos of firefighters pulling victims out of homes.

Over the course of the next two months, the Democrats and labor unions virtually owned the public narrative over Senate Bill 5. With their daily rallies at the Statehouse and complicit JINOs, voters saw compelling images of teachers, firefighters, police officers, and other government workers lamenting the reforms. It was ugly.

The reformers were not aided by the fact that Senate Bill 5 became a "Christmas tree" with dozens of provisions spread out over hundreds of pages. The task of defending Senate Bill 5 would be even harder because, for every provision that polled well, opponents could cite three provisions that polled terribly. More importantly, opponents of Senate Bill 5 successfully defined the legislation as a law that would take away the rights of government workers. Americans instinctively recoil from proposals or laws that take rights away from people.

With complex ballot questions like Senate Bill 5, most voters wouldn't fully understand the legislation, making them more likely to vote against the reforms. The challenge for proponents was to boil the message down to a very clear, simple contrast: higher taxes to maintain the status quo versus government workers living under the same rules as the rest of Ohio.

My Testimony

On February 15, 2011, I testified as an interested party before the Ohio Senate Insurance, Commerce & Labor Committee. After having sat for hours on end, I knew my time was getting close because, about an hour before I was called, Democratic staffers came rushing into the hearing room with copies of "The Grand Bargain" report that compared government compensation packages to the private sector. The Democratic staffers gave their legislators each a copy. The Democrats clearly wanted to take me down.

Just before I was called to testify in the hearing room, roughly 30 burly policemen and firefighters came in and sat down. Here is the testimony I gave that day. You'll recognize some portions of it from earlier passages in this book.

Insurance, Commerce And Labor Committee
Written Statement by Matt A. Mayer
February 15, 2011

Thank you Chairman Bacon, Vice Chair Faber, Ranking Member Schiavone, and Members of this Committee for the opportunity to come before you to provide information concerning the rights of public sector workers to collectively bargain. I am the President of The Buckeye Institute for Public Policy Solutions, a free market research and education think tank. The views I express in this testimony are my own, and should not be construed as representing any official position of The Buckeye Institute.

I'd like to take this opportunity to issue a note of bewilderment. Given some of the rhetoric from my friends on the Left, one would think that this issue—public sector collective bargaining—is a purely illegitimate action to question, a topic unworthy of debate, and something beyond any reasonable person's idea of civilized discussion. As if the rights given through the sheer brute force of a partisan group of politicians in 1983, if taken away in 2011 by similar means, would be tantamount to an unprecedented act in the history of Ohio.

We know there is bipartisan support across Ohio to tweak these rights, including from mayors and other governmental leaders. President Franklin D. Roosevelt and union leaders who really did spill blood to protect workers during the age of sweatshops, unsafe factories, and employer-hired goon violence opposed giving public sector workers the right to collectively bargain.

Are there truly no elements of the current system that the Left will concede need to be reformed? Pay spiking? Double-dipping? Massive sick leave payouts? Pension pick-ups? Longevity pay? COLAs greater than inflation? Highest three-year salary pension formulas? Early retirement? Million dollar secretive retirement programs? As private sector Ohioans suffer, is the status quo for government workers appropriate?

Ohio in 2011 is not America in 1938. Government workers already have the protection of civil service laws. With the proliferation of wage and hour laws, environmental laws, anti-discrimination laws, and other workplace protections that do or easily could protect government workers, is it really that unreasonable to suggest that perhaps adding unions on top is unnecessary and costly? Government offices, precincts, stations, and schools are far from sweatshops and coalmines.

For those same people who advocate for more government, do they not recognize the irony of wanting more of something they believe will mistreat its own workers unless unions were present to keep them at bay? Do they really believe that without unions, voters would stand idly by as leaders abused their neighbors who protect us, teach our children, and provide other necessary government functions? With the proliferation of technologies such as Twitter, cell phone cameras, email, and blogs to add transparency and accountability when the media fail to provide those desperately needed elements, does anyone really believe that but for unions government exempt employees will be able to oppress and mistreat government non-exempt employees?

[According to the Bureau of Labor Statistics,] Ohio can no longer afford the luxury of public sector collective bargaining. From 2000 to today, Ohio's private sector has lost a net of 612,700 jobs. That means there are over 600,000 fewer workers whose activities generated tax revenues to fund government. During that same period of time, Ohio lost a net of only 1,600 government jobs. That means 613,000 fewer workers today are paying for roughly the same size government Ohio had ten years ago in terms of employees. From January 1990 to today, Ohio netted a mere 102,200 private sector jobs and 62,100 government jobs.

As New York Times columnist David Brooks recently wrote [in 'The Freedom Alliance' on February 10, 2011], "The coming budget cuts have nothing to do with merit. They have to do with the inexorable logic of mathematics."

My friends on the Left say that public sector collective bargaining is not the problem. Is that true? With collective bargaining, schools facing fiscal emergencies must cut programs and staff, which only hurts children and younger, but potentially better, teachers. With collective bargaining, the state must cut programs serving the poor and middle class, the group of Ohioans already hit hardest by the economic crisis. With collective bargaining, mayors must cut staffing levels, which undermine our public safety and the careers of young officers and firefighters.

Of course, my friends on the Left have an answer: raise taxes on businesses and rich Ohioans. Ohio already has the seventh highest state and local tax burden and Ohio homeowners already have an average of twenty-five levies on their property. Does any reasonable person really believe that higher taxes and more levies will restore our lost prosperity? In homes across Ohio, reduced incomes mean spending cuts. Why should government be different?

Without collective bargaining, schools, the state, mayors, and other government leaders could make decisions that keep many programs running and staffing at the same level—not one layoff. Would the decisions be painful for government workers? Of course. Would it be more painful than the pain suffered by the 613,000 private sector Ohioans who lost their jobs over the last ten years? Of course, not – not even close. Not to make too fine a point, but any government worker dissatisfied with the new normal can, of course, leave government and find one of those alleged higher paying jobs in the private sector. There are thousands of Ohioans eager to replace them as teachers, police officers, firefighters, and state office workers.

Let me provide this Committee with one example [from the Ohio Department of Administrative Services] of an actual state government worker in a position not requiring a college degree. It shows hidden step and longevity raises significantly increase compensation costs even when pay increases are frozen. Outside of unionized companies, step and longevity increases are not available in the private sector.

As this real example illustrates, in nine years, the position experiences a whopping 55 percent pay increase due to overt yearly salary increases and hidden increases due to steps and longevity pay. This individual did not receive a promotion, so all the increases are due to merely advancing through the system chronologically – six step increases, five salary increases, and three longevity pay increases.

In just nine years, the individual's highest three year salary average went from $31,803 to $45,691, which would result in a first year pension going from $20,990 to $30,156, a 44 percent increase and nearly as much as his first year salary. If this individual retired at age 60, he would receive a lifetime pension of $681,225 – and that is based on just his seventh, eighth, and ninth years of work, not his twenty-eighth, twenty-ninth, and thirtieth years of work.

To be clear, this example is not meant to denigrate the individual. He is merely doing what any Ohioan would do to provide for himself or his family. The same as the 77 Columbus police officers and firefighters who banked years of sick leave—to be used when sick—resulting in payouts as high as $239,829 and averaging $55,607, just for leave not used because those public servants were fortunate to have good health throughout their careers. It is the system that must be reformed to more closely reflect the realities of Ohio's new economic normal.

Let me provide another, broader example. In late October, the 613 school districts submitted their five-year projections to the Ohio Department of Education. The five-year budget projections amounted to a combined deficit in 2015 of more than $7.6 billion. By 2015, compensation costs of teachers, administrators, and staff are projected to swallow 96 percent of all revenue in these districts. So, school districts could devote massive energy to buying cheaper toilet paper, streamlining operations, and reducing other non-compensation costs, but will find themselves nibbling on 4 percent of the remaining revenue.

That means tax increases of nearly $8 billion on homeowners who have seen their homes plummet in value. But, if school districts reduced compensation packages by 10 percent this year, and limited future increases to the historical inflation rate of 3.2 percent, the $7.6 billion shortfall would become a $1 billion surplus. Again, no program cuts and no layoffs. That would enable school districts to soften the impact of expected cuts in state aid to education.

Unfortunately, school districts will not be able to make those realignment reductions because of collective bargaining, as the unions will fight to preserve the gains made over the last decade or more by any means necessary, including hanging out to dry those members who must be the sacrificial lambs so compensation cuts can be prevented.

Like the 4 percent nibbling problem above, eliminating the right to strike and binding arbitration are solid steps, but neither will bend the spending curve down. The fact is roughly 33 percent of all government contracts already involve bargaining units prohibited from striking. Since 2000, [according to the State Employer Relations Board,] Ohio had 10,721 bargained contracts. Of those, 3,487 contracts covered safety units who cannot strike. That leaves 7,234 bargained contracts with strike-eligible units.

Not many have struck. In fact, just 242 notices of intent to strike were issued since 2000, which covers just 3 percent of all contracts. Of those, a mere 43 units, or just over .5 percent, actually struck. Likewise, the contracts that went to fact finding totaled 1,477, or a mere 14 percent. Of those, only 219, or 2 percent, went to binding arbitration. So, eliminating rights not threatened or used very often likely will not result in significant cost savings.

In states that permit government workers to collectively bargain, [the Bureau of Labor Statistics reports that] the average yearly pay for state and local workers is $51,064 and $41,457, respectively. In contrast, in states that prohibit government workers from collectively bargaining, the average yearly pay for state and local workers is $46,025 (11 percent less) and $32,560 (27 percent less), respectively. Perhaps I missed the news stories from those states, but I don't recall reading about government worker violence, mass protests, or rolls of government workers on food stamps. There was not unrest when state workers recently lost the right in Indiana. Pundit beliefs aside, it is not 1978 again. If Ohio paid the 58,000 state workers on average $5,039 less, it would save taxpayers $292,262,000 per year. For local governments, the savings would be even bigger: $5,783,050,000 ($8,897 times 650,000 workers).

Collective bargaining facilitates the explosion of government compensation costs and prohibits governments from making the painful, but necessary, decisions to rein in those costs. It also allows unions to throw roadblocks in the way of reasonable workplace changes and second-guess managers through litigation at every turn, as we saw this past year with the reassignment of police precincts in Columbus.

Private sector Ohioans already carry a heavy burden of taxes, have job prospects grimmer than any time since the Great Depression, have homes continuing to decrease in value, and have retirement accounts hit by the stock market declines. Public sector unions wield enormous power and influence, as the most entrenched interest in America and the single largest spenders on elections in America.

Lessoning the power of public sector union does not mean balancing the budget on the backs of government workers. It just means placing them in the same shoes their private sector neighbors have been walking in for far too long.

Thank you for your time. I am happy to answer questions you might have for me.

Once I completed my testimony, I took questions from the committee. I expected a barrage of questions from the Democratic legislators, but after easily swatting back two questions from two of the Democratic legislators, they apparently decided it might be better to pick on someone less informed. The low point for the Democrats came when Senator Eric Kearney began his questioning of me by trying to tie me to former Secretary of State Ken Blackwell by stating that I worked for him. Following his time as an elected official, Mr. Blackwell served as a fellow at the Buckeye Institute before my tenure. Fair or not, many Ohioans see Mr. Blackwell as a right wing zealot. I had never met Mr. Blackwell, but appreciated his leadership on social issues. Because Senator Kearney couldn't refute the data or my arguments, he resorted to a cheap political stunt by trying to indirectly discredit my testimony and the Buckeye Institute's report by linking me to Mr. Blackwell. It was a shameful display by the now Senate Minority Leader.

As I left the hearing room, the 30 burly unions members got up and walked out with me. A few of the legislators expressed appreciation to me for testifying and for issuing a rebuttal of the union-funded EPI report earlier in the day.

Passage and Months of Silence

On March 2, Senate Bill 5 barely made it out of the Ohio Senate, with only a one-vote majority. I did not provide testimony in the Ohio House. With Senate Bill 5 barely getting out of the Ohio Senate, I knew the Ohio House had to be very careful in what it amended in the legislation.

After roughly one month of hearings, hours of testimony from people on both sides of the issue, and debate among legislators, the Ohio House passed its version of the bill on March 30, 2011, by a 53-44 margin. On March 31, 2011, the Ohio Senate passed the Ohio House version of the bill by a 17-16 margin and, that night, Governor Kasich signed Senate Bill 5 into law.

The labor unions filed the initial 1,000 signatures on April 1, 2011. On April 15, 2011, Secretary of State Jon Husted verified the signatures, thereby starting the 90-day clock to gather the 231,149 signatures required to place the veto referendum on the November 2011 ballot. Not surprisingly, the Democrats and labor unions submitted nearly 1.3 million signatures on June 29, 2011, which set a new record in Ohio. On July 21, 2011, Secretary Husted certified the veto referendum for the November 8, 2011 ballot.

In early May, I met with a top establishment figure to discuss the work we were doing at the Buckeye Institute. During the conversation, I told her about our plan to raise $1.8 million to conduct an education effort on how collective bargaining reforms would keep taxes from getting higher. Our goal was to reach out to 1,000,000 households with easy to understand educational pieces. Given that many Ohioans believed the myth of the underpaid government worker, we thought that it was vital to conduct a broad outreach effort aimed at educating

Ohioans on our work beginning with "The Grand Bargain" report and to let them know about the government salary tools on the Buckeye Institute website.

The Buckeye Institute website had performed exceptionally well in the year since we launched it. From April 30, 2010, to April 30, 2011, over 430,000 visitors from 527 Ohio cities had spent roughly 50,000 hours on the website doing nearly 3,000,000 searches of our government salary tools. While impressive, we knew that these visitors represented only a small fraction of Ohioans. We also knew Ohioans had used the K-12 teacher salary tool to educate voters on teacher salary averages and successfully defeated several proposed school district levies in August 2010 and November 2010. These two data points told us that the more Ohioans knew about these salary tools, the greater chance reformers had of winning any debate over compensation package reforms.

Despite these key facts, I was told to stand down and end my attempts to raise funds for an education outreach effort. I was assured something would be done.

Tragically, nothing happened from May to early September to educate Ohioans on the importance of collective bargaining reform. Instead, the Democrats and the labor unions had the entire summer to communicate their message. During that timeframe, I was bombarded everywhere I went with people asking what the campaign was doing to defend Senate Bill 5. People were eager to help, but had no outlet for their energies. I had to reply that I had no idea since I was not involved with the campaign.

At one point, a Republican House Member in leadership told me that Speaker Batchelder had specifically mentioned during a caucus meeting that he thought I was one of the strongest voices on collective bargaining reform in Ohio and they needed to get me involved in the campaign. I was told to expect a call from him shortly. Despite my offer to take a leave of absence from the Buckeye Institute to barnstorm across Ohio, that call never came because of infighting.

Don't get me wrong, I am not trying to claim that had I barnstormed around Ohio in support of Senate Bill 5 that the results would have been different. I am merely making the point that the reform side had no strategic plan and did no outreach until it was too late. My story is symbolic of this failure and the infighting that has become part and parcel of the Kasich Administration.

The misallocation of precious resources was also a serious problem. "The Grand Bargain" report, which came out in July 2010, exposed the gold-plated government compensation packages compared to the private sector. Professor Matthew Marlin and his team at Duquesne University did the research and wrote the report. Professor Marlin serves as the Chair of the Department of Economics and Statistics and possesses an impeccable reputation. Their conclusion: government workers have compensation packages that cost roughly 28 percent more than their private sector peers.

Instead of promoting that report, the Ohio Business Roundtable spent money to do a duplicative study. They hired Andrew Biggs from the American Enterprise Institute and Jason Richwine, a colleague of mine at The Heritage Foundation. Both Andrew and Jason do great work, and their report was excellent. They took a slightly different approach and included two additional costs that are legitimate issues to consider, but a bit harder to defend; namely, they included the present value of the unfunded aspect of pensions and the "value" of job security. The main conclusion of their report: government workers in Ohio have compensation packages that cost 43 percent more than peers in the private sector. When excluding the two additional factors "The Grand Bargain" report did not include, the cost differential was 31 percent, or just 3 percent higher than the findings in "The Grand Bargain" report.

The political establishment strongly promoted the Biggs-Richwine report, so naturally it received media coverage. The report suffered from two perceptual problems. First, because a business group funded the report, it was marginalized as the report of "hired guns" who arrived at a pre-determined conclusion. This narrative fit perfectly into the talking points of the Democrats and labor unions that Senate Bill 5 was an attack on the middle class. Second, due to the complexity of the arguments, left-wing groups easily raised suspicions about the two additional elements. These two items made the 43 percent differential a bit more difficult to be believe. It just didn't conform to actual data people could access using the Buckeye Institute salary data and comparison tools. This further marginalized the report.

The Democrats and labor unions had the falsely labeled "Rutgers Study" that JINOs promoted without noting it came from a union funded group out of Washington, D.C. The reform side now had two reports with widely "different" results when including the two additional elements. One report was dismissed as a big business funded report. The other report that pre-dated Senate Bill 5 and had strong support among conservative grassroots groups was ignored by the Republican establishment and JINOs.

The point of this anecdote isn't to make the case that the results would have differed if the reform side had gone with "The Grand

Bargain" report; it is to highlight the lack of a strategic plan and the disorganization and fragmentation among proponents of collective bargaining reform. Reformers were split; defenders of the status quo were united.

The Four Keys: Message, Messenger, Organization, and Money

Because the reform side didn't have a strategic plan from the onset, Vaughn Flasher and Jason Mauk, the two talented people charged with running the pro-Senate Bill 5 campaign stood little chance of winning. You can win a campaign with less funding, but you need a critical mass of funding to go with a strong message, messengers, and organization. Vaughn and Jason played catch-up from the beginning and never secured what they needed to win.

Based on my interactions with thousands of Ohioans from across the state, I believe the message should have simply focused on higher taxes versus reform. With 80 percent of school district property tax levies failing in the August 2011 election and the August arrival of bad news from county home appraisals, it seemed to me that Ohioans hated taxes a lot more than they liked protecting the status quo of government workers. The fact that homeowners have filed a record number of tax appeals of their county home appraisals is strong proof that the higher taxes versus reform message could have been a winner. Yet, the reform message focused on aspects of Senate Bill 5, subjecting it to death by a thousand cuts as the other side pointed at other provisions that people didn't like.

As Senate Bill 5 went down in flames by 62 percent, these same voters rejected 78 percent of the local levies on the ballot. Many of those voters failed to make the connection between the need for those levies (higher taxes) <u>because of</u> the pro-union collective bargaining law in Ohio. Had the reform message properly connected the two, I am confident the results would have been far different. Again, the reformers may not have won, but it would not have been the shellacking it was that has now resulted in a timid legislature and a steeper hill for passing a workplace freedom law in Ohio.

The reform side did not have a good messenger. News accounts reported that pollster Frank Luntz had conducted focus groups around Ohio on Senate Bill 5 and found that Governor Kasich's low approval ratings and his style of communicating made him toxic to the campaign. He was advised to stay away from the campaign. Unfortunately, he didn't. As he showed up on the front page of newspapers and in television reports talking about Senate Bill 5, polling data worsened.

In early October, the anti-reform campaign ran an effective ad featuring Marlene Quinn, a great grandmother, talking about how firefighters pulled her granddaughter Zoey out of a burning house. In the ad, Ms. Quinn stated

> If not for the firefighters, we wouldn't have our Zoey today. I don't want the politicians in Columbus making decisions for the firefighters, the police, teachers, nurses, or any organization that's helping people. Fewer firefighters could mean the difference between life or death — and that's why I'm voting 'No' on Issue 2.

The reform side used Ms. Quinn's first sentence in a response ad and added an announcer stating "She's RIGHT — by voting 'No' on Issue 2, our safety will be threatened. Without Issue 2, communities will need to lay off hard-working firefighters, to pay for the excessive benefits of other government employees." The anti-reform campaign quickly rolled out Ms. Quinn again to chastise the reform side for misappropriating her image and words to mislead viewers about her stance on Senate Bill 5. JINOs covered the flap extensively allowing Ms. Quinn to eviscerate the reform side.

Reformers also were beaten on organization. Building a Better Ohio simply did not have enough time to put in place the organization and ground game needed to counter the finely-tuned labor union machine. Reforming collective bargaining was a threat to the existence and power of government labor unions. Those groups, in Ohio and nationally, left no stone unturned to defeat the reforms.

In my role, I spent a lot of time driving around Ohio educating thousands of Ohioans on the fiscal crisis we faced. I knew the campaign was not going well. Everywhere I drove, I saw yard signs opposing Senate Bill 5 and rarely came across a pro-reform sign. In meetings, I was constantly asked where people could get yard signs. The Buckeye Institute received emails, telephone calls, and in-person requests to come speak on behalf of Senate Bill 5, but could only refer them to the Building a Better Ohio campaign given the Buckeye Institute's non-advocacy status. They would respond, "Yeah, we've called and sent emails, but no one has responded."

Regardless of funding, the reform side had a muddled message, no strong messenger, and a weak organization. Building a Better Ohio managed to raise roughly $12 million and ended up being badly outspent by the $42 million raised by Democrats and labor unions. Interestingly, despite the tens of millions of dollars spent by Democrats and labor unions, the opposition to Senate Bill 5 didn't change much from the initial polling in February 2011. The reformers and taxpayers didn't stand a chance.

One of the problems I heard time and time again focused on the near constant request from entities on the right for money from conservative donors. Those donors had contributed significant amounts of funding to win the November 2010 election. They got the results they wanted when Republicans won virtually every key race in Ohio.

Shortly thereafter, those same conservative donors were called upon to fund numerous separate efforts. These efforts included Governor Kasich's inauguration, the group One Ohio United that he launched to defend his biennial budget, and his new JobsOhio economic development idea. One Ohio United spent millions defending Governor Kasich's budget as no funds were spent promoting the Senate Bill 5 reforms. These donors also received fund raising requests from the Koch brothers and Karl Rove, as well as many other non-Ohio entities such as FreedomWorks, Americans for Prosperity, and American Majority. When it came to Senate Bill 5, because the case had not been made on why the reforms were critical to fixing Ohio, the exhausted conservative donor base declined to support the effort. The work of all of these causes is important, but you can only get so much water from the well before the well runs dry.

Even tactical decisions appeared to lack real strategic thought. Shortly before the deadline to withdraw the veto referendum from the ballot passed, Governor Kasich and legislative leaders offered to sit down with the Democrats and the labor unions to discuss amendments to Senate Bill 5 that they would make in exchange for withdrawing the veto referendum. At the time, the external polling data showed strong support for the anti-Senate Bill 5 effort. Though not public, Governor Kasich and the legislative leaders had to know that fundraising was not going well, either. These two realities meant that the Democrats and labor unions had no motive to come to the table to negotiate. Governor Kasich was operating from a position of weakness, and everyone seemed to know it.

From a strategic standpoint, Governor Kasich needed to change the dynamic and create uncertainty for the Democrats and labor unions. Instead of a blanket offer to negotiate, Governor Kasich and the legislative leaders could have said that, if the Senate Bill 5 reforms went down on November 8, within 30 days, the Republicans would enact single subject pieces of legislation on all the provisions both sides knew had the support of a majority of Ohioans. These items included elimination of teacher tenure, requiring government workers to cover at least 15 percent of their health care policy costs, elimination of longevity bonuses, elimination of step increases, and elimination of sick leave banking. Governor Kasich could have noted that he had already polled the Republican legislators and had more than enough votes to pass each of these pieces of legislation.

Without a tactical move that created uncertainty for the other side and broadened the field of play beyond the November 8 election, the gambit looked like a public relations move to curry the favor of key editorial boards. The Democrats and labor unions didn't show up at the meeting place to negotiate with Republican leaders, and the withdrawal deadline passed. Grassroots activists for reform, who had been told the polling and funding looked good, reacted with varying amounts of frustration, disappointment, and, for the first time, doubt. Even worse, focus groups showed that voters saw Governor Kasich's move as "fake" and "staged," which further negatively impacted their views of him.

A week or so after Labor Day, the first Building a Better Ohio direct mail piece in support of Senate Bill 5 hit homes. This piece was the first communication Ohioans had received from the pro-Senate Bill 5 side. For the remainder of the election season, Ohioans were inundated with television and direct mail ads from groups opposing Senate Bill 5. The number of ads from the reform side paled in comparison. Surprisingly, despite the widespread knowledge about the significant use of the Buckeye Institute government salary data tools, not once did Building a Better Ohio direct voters to the tools to see, as the *Dispatch* editorial board said, the gold-plated compensation packages for themselves.

On November 8, 2011, the collective bargaining reforms died. The veto referendum passed with 62 percent of the vote.

Making Lemonade Out of Lemons

On November 9, 2011, the fiscal crises facing thousands of Ohio local government entities was still there. In fact, because 78 percent of the levies on local ballots failed, the fiscal condition of many local government entities got worse. Governor Kasich and the Republican legislators did nothing to help alleviate these crises.

I would submit that they had an option. They could have forced the Democrats and labor unions leaders to walk the talk.

Over the course of the Senate Bill 5 debate, the Democrats and labor unions called the legislation extreme. They agreed that reforms were necessary, but rejected Senate Bill 5 as too radical. Governor Kasich and the Republican legislators could have held a press conference after the November 8 defeat to highlight some of the statements made by opponents about "reasonable reforms." They could have said they would eagerly work with Democrats and the labor unions to enact the reforms they had affirmed. But they didn't.

Here are a few examples of the pro-reform statements that could have been mentioned:

- During a debate on the *Sean Hannity Show* on October 26, 2011, Sean Hannity and Democratic Senator Joe Schiavoni had this exchange:
  - Hannity: "What's wrong with the contribution aspect that we just mentioned (10 percent pension, 15 percent health care), do you have a problem with that?"
  - Schiavoni: "No, and if that was the bill, that would be the discussion."
- In a *Dispatch* article from February 17, 2011, reporter Jim Siegel reported that during his testimony, "Mark Sanders, president of the Ohio Association of Professional Firefighters, said a review of the law may be justified, and he does not object to attempts to make bargaining more transparent."
- In the same article, Siegel noted: "Sen. Tom Sawyer, D-Akron, told Berding that collective bargaining was implemented to avoid the numerous public worker strikes that were occurring, and it has worked. While things need refining, 'clearly this is not a system that is as broken as the system that preceded it.'"
- In the February 18, 2011 "Statehouse Update" by the Ohio Township Association, in response to Toledo Deputy Mayor Stephen Herwat's testimony in support of Senate Bill 5, Democratic Senator Tom Sawyer replied, "Maybe there are refinements that need to be made. Thank you for your testimony. It certainly sounds a lot better than throwing the whole baby out with the bath water."
- In his testimony to the Ohio Senate Insurance, Commerce, and Labor Committee, Jay McDonald, Ohio Fraternal Order of Police President, stated: "The Fraternal Order of Police of Ohio recognizes that collective bargaining laws have remained largely unchanged since 1984. Refinements may be necessary to update the current law, and we stand ready and willing to work with all of you in that process."
- Finally, it was implicit in the Democrats' and labor unions' offer to negotiate collective bargaining reforms if Republicans repealed Senate Bill 5 that they acknowledged the need for reforms. Otherwise, why offer to negotiate reforms at all?

Governor Kasich and the Republican legislators could have requested the Democrats and the labor unions to offer specific "reasonable reforms" so Ohio's local governments could more easily manage their fiscal crises.

Had they made this offer, two outcomes would have been possible. Either the Democrats and labor unions would have stuck to their words and offered reasonable reforms to the 28 year old collective bargaining law or they would have revealed themselves to be liars and frauds. Regardless, as of the printing of this book, the Democrats and the labor unions have still not offered a single statewide reform of Ohio's collective bargaining law.

This failure would not surprise anyone. The Democrats have a long track record of protecting the status quo on collective bargaining. They opposed Governor Voinovich's minor change to the definition of inherent management rights in 1995. They showed resistance to reform when they controlled the Governor's Office and the Ohio House from 2008 to 2010. Facing fiscal crises across Ohio, Governor Strickland and Speaker Armond Budish had the opportunity to amend the law with whatever "reasonable" reforms they felt needed to be made to improve the law.

Finally, throughout the entire Senate Bill 5 legislative process, the Democrats did not offer a single amendment in either the Ohio Senate or the Ohio House. Their only offer of "compromise" consisted of a demand to repeal Senate Bill 5 before they would discuss reforms. Democrats and labor unions made this demand from a position of strength given the polling data showing them well ahead. They also made this demand and their comments acknowledging the need for reforms knowing that no one, especially the JINOs, would hold them accountable for their statements.

[JINO Alert #5: Media outlets should follow-up with the Democrats and labor unions to see what their plans are to enact "reasonable reforms" to Ohio's collective bargaining law.]

In other states, the connection between the Democratic Party and labor unions is strong, but Democrats outside of Ohio sometimes buck the labor unions. For example, Rhode Island Democrats did on government pension reform in 2012. But in Ohio, the labor unions own the Democratic Party and get exactly what they want from it. There is not one major issue in Ohio where a majority of Democrats voted against the position of labor unions. Ohio taxpayers get stuck with the bill for this costly alliance.

Leaders Lead, Typical Politicians "Move On"

On June 5, 2012, Wisconsin voters confirmed their decision to hire Scott Walker as Governor by soundly rejecting the labor union's recall effort. From beginning to end, Governor Walker never waivered on the importance of Wisconsin's collective bargaining reforms. Without a doubt, Governor Walker went all in to pass and defend his legislation that dramatically changed public sector collective bargain in Wisconsin. Interestingly, though Governor Walker did not gain much support from union members (29 percent), he did gain significant support from voters who live with union members (48 percent), thereby indicating that even union household will support labor union reforms.

In Ohio, as highlighted previously, Governor Kasich did not

campaign on the issue of collective bargaining reform. Upon becoming governor, he did not issue an executive order reversing Governor Strickland's executive order unionizing home health care and day care workers. In facing a projected $8 billion deficit, he did not declare exigent circumstances and unilaterally reform state government compensation packages. In defending his staff pay, he took the position that government workers should be paid generously. Finally, after the defeat of Senate Bill 5, he cut a deal with state workers that provided them $21 million a year in pay increases.

In terms of Senate Bill 5, Governor Kasich repeatedly tried to disclaim ownership of the collective bargaining reform legislation. Specifically, Governor Kasich spent the spring making sure that people knew the Senate Bill 5 was not his legislation. In an interview on CNN about Senate Bill 5 on February 22, 2011, when the reporter asked him about "his proposal," Governor Kasich quickly responded by stating "Well, wait, wait, first of all, first of all Jessica, Senator Jones' bill is not my bill."

Then, on March 8, 2011, Governor Kasich delivered his 2011 State of the State address to the Ohio legislature. This vital first address to Ohioans occurred one week after Senate Bill 5 barely made it out of the Ohio Senate by one vote. In 17 pages of remarks, here is the sum total of what Governor Kasich had to say on the issue of collective bargaining reform:

> And, frankly, folks, the provisions of collective bargaining reform are examples of what we wanted to do to allow people to be able to control their costs. And by the way, I appreciate the passion of people that don't agree with us, you know? I grew up in the '70s. I learned what protests were in the '70s. I understand it. And people who are strongly – people who feel strongly, I respect them.

He could have spent a few pages laying out the case for why collective bargaining reforms were critical to fixing Ohio.

Finally, two weeks after the labor unions submitted signatures to start the clock on qualifying for the veto referendum, in an interview with a *Dispatch* reporter on April 24, 2011, he indicated that Senator Jones had "jumped the gun" and that he had preferred a different approach to the issue.

Beyond the spring, Governor Kasich's team privately alleged that Senate Bill 5 was a nefarious conspiracy concocted by his archrival Republican Secretary of State Jon Husted and Husted loyalist Senator Jones to undermine Governor Kasich. The conspiracy theory focused on weakening Governor Kasich so he either wouldn't run for reelection in 2014 or would be susceptible to a primary challenge by Secretary Husted. The bitterness between Governor Kasich and Secretary Husted played out in 2012 with Governor Kasich's successful effort to oust Husted ally Kevin DeWine as the Chairman of the Ohio Republican Party.

Once it was clear that the success or failure of Senate Bill 5 would be tied around his political neck, to his credit, Governor Kasich went to work defending the legislation. As noted above, however, Governor Kasich did not have an end-to-end strategy to pass and to defend the reforms. Thus, unlike Governor Walker, Governor Kasich was not prepared to win the war and the fundraising, organization, and messaging demonstrated this fundamental weakness.

When asked about Governor Walker's victory on June 5, 2012, and what that victory meant in Ohio, Governor Kasich noted the people had spoken and that "we've moved on." He may have moved on, but the fiscal crisis in local governments across Ohio did not.

Increasingly, that crisis is being placed on the backs of Ohioans. Once again, taxpayers don't stand a chance in Ohio. If the Governor of Ohio doesn't want to deal with the problem, who will?

7

THE LOCAL PROPETY TAX ASSAULT: LEVY FATIGUE AND EMOTIONAL BLACKMAIL

"57 percent of new levies passed."

Ohioans live with a basic reality. First, state government spending exceeds inflation and population growth year after year no matter who runs our government. While certain taxes may get lowered, other taxes and fees rise to feed general revenue fund expenditure growth. Ohioans, directly or indirectly, end up paying the bill.

Secondly, most school districts and other local government entities whose revenue comes from property taxes typically predict that compensation package costs, the single largest component of local budgets, will rise roughly 5 percent or more year after year. This means that property taxes must inevitably rise to cover these generous compensation package increases.

Thirdly, local income taxes rarely, if ever, get lowered. In fact, just the opposite is the trend. Local governments constantly seek higher income taxes.

Finally, most importantly, Ohioans already provide state and local governments with a generous level of tax revenue that should cover the cost of providing necessary government goods and services. Ohio does not suffer from a lack of revenue. If state and local governments had restrained spending even just a bit over the last two decades, those entities would not need another dime of tax revenue.

For example, as highlighted in the "Six Principles for Fixing Ohio" report, had state general revenue fund expenditures grown at the same pace as our population and inflation combined, that component of Ohio's budget would be just over $21 billion in 2012. Instead, it is estimated to come in at more than $27 billion in 2012 and over $28 million in 2013. Even at $24 billion, the current tax revenues would more than adequately cover the bill.

Similarly, if school districts and other local government entities limited compensation package cost increases to inflation, then the need for additional tax revenue would be significantly reduced or even eliminated. For example, if Ohio's school districts would have instituted an across-the-board 10 percent compensation package reduction in 2010 and limited future growth to Ohio's historical inflation rate of 3.2 percent, the $7.6 billion deficit would become a nearly $1 billion surplus. In the worst case, those entities would not need as much revenue from new levies as currently needed or need new levies so frequently, thereby limiting property tax growth.

It's Not a Fair Fight

Even without the free media local governments get from JINOs as described in Chapter 4, taxpayers are at an enormous disadvantage when it comes to stopping tax hikes. First, taxpayers don't possess the data on spending and compensation package increases. Because local government entities control the data, they can present the data in the best possible light.

For example, taxpayers routinely hear that their school district has cut spending by a specific figure. That claim is typically not true because the cut is a reduction in future spending that is still more than the previous or current year's budget. An example is freezing step increases but still giving base salary pay and longevity pay increases. Or it is a savings derived from not doing something in the future such as not filing a vacancy or not building a new school building. Rarely, if ever, is the cut a reduction in spending below the level of previous spending.

Without easy voter or citizen access to data, government leaders promote statistics and facts that hide that truth behind their need for more money.

For most tax levies on the ballot, there is no formal opposition. So taxpayers only hear one side of the story. The reason formal opposition rarely occurs rests in the fact that the cost of opposing is higher than the cost of doing nothing. Let me explain.

In addition to the time commitment needed to effectively oppose a levy, the out-of-pocket expenses would be high. These costs would include securing a web domain name, server space, building a website, complying with campaign finance laws, developing campaign material, and, most expensively, printing and distributing material to voters. Even if an individual could produce a campaign piece to send to voters inexpensively, the printing and postage cost to mail the piece to voters would run, at a minimum, 40 cents per piece. For a jurisdiction with just 5,000 homes, one mailing would cost roughly $2,000.

Compare that cost with the impact the passed levy would have on taxes. If the levy would add $150 to an individual's property taxes for every $100,000 in his home's value, it would take a fairly expensive home to justify spending $2,000 on one campaign mailer (exclusive of the other costs mentioned). Even when considering the multi-year impact of the tax, the home still would need to be expensive to justify the campaign expenses.

Of course, as the number of individuals contributing to the opposition campaign increase, the per individual cost would decrease. That means the economic justification for taking action would increase. Finding a handful of individuals willing to spend $500 to oppose a property tax levy is easier in a wealthier area, but other aspects undermine gathering such support.

One aspect is that there is widespread belief that publicly opposing a levy will result in being blackballed in the community. Business owners fear being targeted, which is what happened during California's Proposition 8 campaign. Individuals also fear being stigmatized by neighbors and friends. I've had people tell me their husbands or wives told them to keep quiet about a proposed levy because they had friends who worked for a government unit.

More troubling, one individual told me about being approached at a business group meeting by a local government leader. The government leader let the individual know that he did not appreciate comments made at a recent public event. Just to make sure the individual got his message, the government leader noted that he knew that the individual's child took a certain high school class, a fact he wouldn't know unless he looked into the classes the individual's kid took. This individual, to protect his child, altered his future activities.

People with children also fear that teachers will target their children if they speak out against a levy. Having publicly opposed levies personally and having been involved in public work for the Buckeye Institute, I have never felt that a teacher took action against my kids for my work. I believe government workers, especially teachers, are far too professional to do that. Nonetheless, I have received emails from and had conversations with other people in which they fear their kids would be targeted by teachers if they spoke up. As the saying goes, perception is reality.

But, even if you can find a group of fellow citizens willing to spend their hard-earned money to successfully fight a levy and who dismiss the blackballing threat that might be visited upon them, their businesses, or their children, another more vexing and, ultimately, deadly fact remains. Levy proponents get as many bites at the apple as they want in Ohio. It only takes 50 percent of the vote plus one more vote to pass the levy. Thus, these citizens need to be willing to fund opposition campaigns every time the levy is placed on the ballot. The marginal costs rise with each opposition campaign, thereby making the cost-benefit analysis far less compelling. In Ohio, a levy can be run at least three times per year.

It is a permanent fight that eventually overwhelms even the most concerned citizens. This levy fatigue makes it all but certain that most local tax issues will succeed.

They Threaten Us with Emotional Blackmail

Local governments are successful in passing tax hikes because they hold all the power. But wait, you are saying, we get to vote and that means we have the power. If the process only worked that way, then maybe things would be different.

As discussed in Chapter 4, local government entities get an

enormous amount of free media in the form of weekly columns and uncritical news stories. They also routinely use the tax dollars we provide them to promote levies. This promotion comes in many forms and usually avoids using the words "Vote for the levy," but it happens all the time and, unfortunately, is perfectly legal.

In the fall of 2011, Dublin City Schools attempted to pass a levy that would have substantially increased school property taxes on homeowners. During the campaign, Dublin City Schools repeatedly pushed the limit on using property taxes in support of the levy. The *Dispatch* carried a news story, "Schools walk fine line on levy," detailing the activities Dublin and Westerville City Schools engaged in as part of their levy campaigns. The October 16, 2011 *Dispatch* story noted:

> State law forbids school districts from spending taxpayer money to support or oppose a tax request, but it allows them to use public resources to communicate information about "plans, policies and operations."
>
> Legal experts said it's a blurry line that becomes blurrier when schools spread information about levy plans that some could see as thinly veiled requests to vote yes.
>
> Dublin school officials have spent about $8,500 to publicize information about the district's Nov. 8 ballot request for a combined tax issue. Signs outside each school building, saying what the issue would provide, cost about $4,500, and letters to voters cost about $4,000, officials said.

Later, on October 21, 2011, the *Dispatch* ran an editorial titled, "Stay in bounds: School districts that go too far in pushing levies face pushback," stating:

> Allowing schools to communicate with voters about the

levy request is essential if voters are to make an informed choice. But, as public resources, school lawns and meeting rooms should be as available to anti-levy groups as they are to pro-levy ones.

Another safeguard against abuse is the fact that school districts that push their message too heavy-handedly might lose votes. They open themselves to criticism from opponents and could alienate those on the fence about a levy.

Voters and parents, especially, dislike seeing children used in levy campaigns, whether as PR props or actual labor. Dublin Coffman High School Athletic Director Tony Pusateri sent an email to coaches asking, "please try to get your teams to participate" in a pro-levy envelope-stuffing event.

Such communications always are shared and seen by people other than the initial list of recipients, and some are bound to be offended when it appears that a line was crossed.

In addition to those items detailed by the *Dispatch*, Dublin City Schools used property tax money to make a video to play during curriculum night promoting the levy and to send out pro-levy messages from the parent support groups.

As highlighted in Chapter 4, according to the campaign finance reports at the Franklin County Board of Elections and the 2010-2011 list of Dublin City Schools vendors, funds from vendors, who received over $12 million in payments, and school district employees covered the entire $41,000 spent by the Good Schools Committee on the campaign.

These types of activities and funding shenanigans occur across Ohio and in other states during every levy campaign.

To pass a tax hike, local governments just need 50 percent of the voters to agree plus one more voter. Though I don't know what the percentage is, every community has Joe and Jane do-gooders who vote in support of higher taxes (I mean, in support of government) no matter what the issue is, as well as those who directly will gain financially from the tax increase such as vendors, teachers, firefighters, police officers, and city workers. These are the base tax hike supporters.

On top of this base are the voters who approach voting as if it were a vote for the high school prom king and queen. These voters are the ones who uncritically accept the messages from the government tax proponent that supporting the levy is really about supporting the kids or the teachers or our public safety forces. Who doesn't want to support those groups? Even I want to be part of that team. Certainly, no one wants to be known as someone on the other side who doesn't support the children or teachers, right?

Emotional blackmail plays its role in pushing uncertain voters over the edge. The emotional blackmail hits many hot button issues for residents. For parents focused on the academic aspect of their children's education, the school districts threaten to cancel advanced placement and language classes or enlarge class sizes. For parents focused on athletics, they threaten to eliminate sports or charge players for participating. For parents of students with other skills, they threaten to cancel band, art, and theater. For parents with struggling or special needs students, they threaten tutor and extra support programs.

As noted in Chapter 4, one story highlighted potential cuts that would occur if the 2011 Dublin levy did not pass. The story noted:

> Superintendent David Axner said the district would have 25 students in kindergarten and first-grade classes, 27 students in grades 2 and 3, and 30 students in grades 4 and 5. In the middle and high schools, classes would carry a 30-1 student-to-teacher ratio, he said. Other areas facing potential cuts include supplemental contracts, stipends, professional development, field trips, maintenance, reading support, educational options and busing.

Superintendent Axner left virtually nothing off the table. Two months after the levy defeat, *This Week* continued to push the school district's message of cuts to programs and staffing. With new teacher and staff contract negotiations beginning in the next year when voters will consider a second levy request, *This Week* fails to report on what compensation package reductions, if any, Superintendent Axner will request from the labor unions. Because such information isn't reported by JINOs, it appears they never even ask if base compensation cuts will be part of the budget deficit solution. These program and staffing threats are not just idly made. They work.

In the fall of 2011, Westerville City Schools placed a combined levy-income tax increase on the ballot. The package would have resulted in Westerville residents paying $124.34 more per $100,000 in assessed home value, as well as a half percent on all income. A small, but vocal group engaged in education activities in opposition to the levy-income tax package. Westerville voters rejected the levy-income tax package with 61 percent of the vote.

Undaunted, Westerville City Schools spent the next three months threatening residents with details of all the cuts to programs and all the additional fees that would be levied against students unless voters approved a levy in March 2012. Westerville City Schools eliminated the income tax hike and proposed a levy that would add $211.00 to school property taxes for every $100,000 in assessed home value.

To show voters that they had gotten the message and to increase the odds of passage, Westerville City Schools asked the various government unions representing teachers and other workers to agree to concessions prior to the March 2012 vote. The requested concessions consisted of a two-year wage freeze and paying for higher health care premiums. The Westerville Education Association, betting the emotional blackmail had worked, refused to agree to the concessions.

Their bet paid off, as Westerville voters passed the levy with 51 percent of the vote, or by just 585 votes. Unlike the 80 percent rejection rate for levies in August 2011 and the 78 percent rejection rate for levies in November 2011, Ohio voters approved 57 percent of levy increases and 75 percent of all levies (renewal and new) in March 2012, which is the highest approval percentage since November 2000.

As the *Dispatch* reported on March 8, 2012, in "Voters were sympathetic to schools' levy requests," "In Westerville and other parts of the state, voters opened their wallets in the wake of sweeping cuts in state aid to schools last year." The cuts were part of Governor Kasich's 2012-2013 budget. Because Governor Kasich did not use the funds to lower state income taxes, but instead used the funds to eliminate the deficit (instead of spending cuts), it was fairly obvious that the net impact of the cuts on Ohioans would be higher taxes once local levy increases replaced the funds Kasich appropriated.

In addition to school district tax levy increases, townships also are seeking higher taxes to replace the state budget cuts. As the *Dispatch* reported on February 10, 2011, in "Kasich of little cheer to township trustees," townships placed "more than 1,000 township tax issues on the November ballot last year; 80 percent passed." Ohioans are, as the cliché goes, dying a death by a 1,000 local tax hikes.

In local governments across Ohio, voters are always presented a false choice: either vote for higher taxes or endure program and service cuts (i.e., emotional blackmail). There is a third choice that would allow local government to live within the generous revenues already provided by taxpayers. This third choice also would prevent program and service cuts, including layoffs of good teachers, police officers, firefighters, and other government workers. This third choice, however, is never on the table because of the power of labor unions.

Ironically, the government labor unions would rather lose a few members and their dues as a result of layoffs than accept broad base pay reductions. It is all about the money.

According to the Ohio Education Association's (OEA) 2011-2012 Local Association Membership Enrollment Manual,

> Annual OEA dues of active members who are educators (such as classroom teachers, professors, school nurses, pupil personnel workers) shall be .0076 per dollar *of the average salary for elementary and secondary classroom teachers in Ohio* for the second year prior to the budget year rounded to the nearest dollar. An additional service fee shall be .0010 per dollar *of the average salary for elementary and secondary public school classroom teachers in Ohio* for the 2009-2010 year rounded to the nearest dollar. (emphasis added).

The total dues owed by each full-time teacher in Ohio ranges from $742.00 for teachers in the Western OEA district to $764.50 for teachers in the Central OEA district. That figure includes the OEA dues ($479.00), a service charge ($76.00), the National Education

Association dues ($178.00), and the district dues ($9.00 to $31.50).

Because the government labor unions calculate their dues based upon the average salary of members, broad base pay reductions result in a loss of funding that is greater than the losses due to layoffs. For example, the current dues rate of $479.00 translates to an average salary for teachers in Ohio of $63,026.32. If that average salary dropped due to base pay reductions to $62,000, the OEA dues would drop to $471.20 (or $7.80 less) per member. Assuming just 100,000 of the OEA's 130,000 members are full-time teachers, this reduction would translate into the OEA losing roughly $780,000 per year. To reach a similar loss of dues via layoffs, school districts would need to layoff over 1,600 teachers ($479.00 annual dues x 1,628 lost members = $779,812). From 2001 to 2011, despite educating over 100,000 fewer students, the number of full-time teachers in Ohio only dropped by roughly 6,000 teachers (or less than 600 per year). So while layoffs may occur in a few school districts across Ohio, the trend does not suggest 1,600 layoffs per year. Thus, it should be no surprise that labor unions will sacrifice a few members to preserve the base pay of the many.

The third choice that exists for taxpayers is for workers to accept across the board compensation package reductions. Compensation packages cuts are quite familiar in the private sector. Why should government be immune from these actions when times are tough? This third option should be part of the discussion.

As noted in the "Six Principles for Fixing Ohio" report, according to the financial reports submitted to the Ohio Department of Education in October 2010, Ohio's school districts projected an aggregate deficit in 2015 of $7.6 billion with 96 percent of all tax revenue going to compensation package costs. Compensation package costs in some school districts substantially exceeded 100 percent of all tax revenue. If school districts would have instituted an across-the-board 10 percent compensation package reduction in 2010 and limited future growth to 3.2 percent (Ohio's historical inflation rate), the $7.6 billion deficit would become a nearly $1 billion surplus and would have avoided nearly $8 billion in property tax increases.

Taxpayers cannot keep up with the unsustainable pace of cost increases in Ohio. Per pupil expenditures increased from $7,178 in 2000 to $10,128 in 2010, a 41.1 percent increase. Not surprisingly, the average teacher pay jumped from $40,031 in 2000 to $53,156 in 2010, a 33 percent increase. In Dublin City Schools, average teacher salaries skyrocketed by 47 percent.

As costs have gone up significantly, the educational outcomes in Ohio have made little progress as measured by results on the National Assessment of Education Progress (NAEP). For eighth graders, the average NAEP score in math went up from 281 in 2000 to 289 in 2011 and the average NAEP score in reading stayed at 268 from 2002 to 2011. The percentage of eighth graders performing at or above the proficient level in math increased from 30 percent in 2000 to 39 percent in 2011. In reading, those students at or above the proficient level increased by just two percent, with only 37 percent of students hitting that mark.

At the same time, the *Beacon-Journal* reported in August 2011 that for Ohio students who attend college, "42 percent of full-time students at public colleges and universities take at least one remedial course in English or basic math to prepare them for college-level work." The *Blade* also reported in August 2011 that:

Results of ACT college-admission tests suggest that nearly three-quarters of Ohio high school graduates aren't completely prepared for college. Test results released Wednesday show that only 28 percent of test-takers in the Class of 2011 at Ohio public and private high schools met college readiness standards in English, reading, math and science.

In "Building a Grad Nation: Progress and Challenge in Ending the High School Dropout Epidemic," an annual report produced jointly by four groups, Ohio's 2002 graduation rate was 77.5 percent. Even though per pupil spending increased substantially, the graduation rate seven years later in 2009 had only improved by 2.1 percent.

Ohio's soft grading system for schools results in report cards totally out-of-whack with the NAEP, ACT, remedial education needs, and dropout rate. Currently, 2,608 schools, or 77 percent of all Ohio schools, receive a grade of "Effective" or higher. A stunning 1,768 schools received an "Excellent" or "Excellent with Distinction" grade. Only 362 schools received an "Academic Watch" or "Academic Emergency" rating. Governor Kasich's proposal to strengthen the school grading system is an excellent step in the right direction.

With the mediocre results achieved over the last decade despite the large jumps in expenditures and teacher compensation, taxpayers deserve a break from the ever-increasing tax burden and the emotional blackmail. Enough is enough! Without fundamental government compensation package reforms, they won't get that break.

8

RADICAL IN 2012: FORCED UNIONIZATION

AFGE Union Boss John Cage: "When people say 'well we just have to pay less in wages' whether it's in the private sector or public sector, I think they're mentally retarded."

Let's do a simple thought exercise. Pretend that you are the Platonic Philosopher King of Ohio and get to decide whether Ohio is a forced unionization state or a workplace freedom state. Today is the first day of the state's existence.

There is one twist, however, to this blank slate. It isn't exactly blank. There are already laws in place. These laws include the following laws and protections:

- Federal and state unemployment insurance;
- State workers' compensation protections;
- Federal and state age discrimination protections;
- Federal and state sex discrimination protections;
- Federal and state race discrimination protections;
- Federal and state gender discrimination protections;
- Federal and state national origin discrimination protections;
- Federal and state disabilities discrimination protections;
- Federal and state whistleblower protections;
- Federal and state retaliation protections;
- Family Medical Leave Act protections;

- Employee Polygraph Protection Act protections;
- Equal Pay Act protections;
- Rehabilitation Act protections;
- Fair Labor Standards Act protections;
- Lilly Ledbetter Fair Pay Act protections;
- Electronic Communications Privacy Act protections;
- State and local sexual orientation protections;
- Occupational Safety & Health Act protections;
- Clean Air Act protections;
- Commercial Motor Vehicle Safety Act protections;
- Congressional Accountability Act protections;
- False Claims Act protections;
- Federal Mine Safety & Health Act protections;
- Migrant Seasonal & Agricultural Worker Protection Act protections;
- Railroad Safety Act protections;
- Safe Drinking Water Act protections;
- Federal Section 1981 and Section 1985 protections;
- Employee Retirement Income Security Act protections;
- Worker Adjustment & Retraining Notification Act protections;
- Various federal asbestos protections;
- Federal and state wage and hour protections;
- Common law tort, libel, slander, and negligent or intentional infliction of emotional distress protections;
- Minimum wage requirements; and
- Civil service protections (for government workers).

On top of these legal protections, local laws also provide additional protections. Even more important are the non-legal protections provided to workers today due to the prevalence of transparency tools such as video cell phones, Twitter, Facebook, YouTube, and other social media tools workers can use to publicize unfair or wrongful treatment.

The Benefits of Labor Unions in 2012

Any discussion on the value of labor unions must begin with an acknowledgement of the historical importance of labor unions in America. Labor unions deserve credit for dramatically altering the American workplace.

The bulk of that good work occurred from 1900 to 1950, as the pressure from labor unions led to significant improvements in the safety and condition of the workplace and the protections and compensation provided to workers. As with other movements, however, labor unions moved from truly improving the workplace to focusing on items that impact their financial bottom lines. First, labor unions drive compensation packages as high as possible for members. Second, they push for more workers by injecting inefficiencies into the system with rigid work rules. Last, labor unions protect weak or bad employees no matter the case against those employees.

With the devastation in continental Europe and Japan in World War II, labor unions in America could get away with these three goals because global competition was weak or non-existent thereby allowing American companies to "spread the wealth" around. This deal between corporate America and labor unions created artificially high compensation packages—artificial because those packages were disconnected from a competitive marketplace.

As Europe and Japan recovered from the destruction of World War II and developing or under developed countries increasingly entered the global marketplace, unionized American companies found it harder and harder to compete. The car industry is the most visible example of this dynamic. It is not surprising then that the unionization rate in the United States declined from roughly 36 percent in 1970 down to 12 percent today. This decline has occurred despite the continued existence of pro-labor union federal and state laws, especially for government workers.

Though the private sector has had to adjust to the new economic reality brought on by a globally competitive marketplace, state and local governments remain tied to the blue social model of the New Deal.

In addition to compensation packages out of touch with economic reality, labor unions also inhibit workplace flexibility due to byzantine work rules and the ability of workers to file countless grievances and unfair labor practice charges against their employers, as highlighted below with the Hostess Brands bankruptcy. Despite the media attention given to the compensation cost issues, for many employers, the burden of labor unions rests more with the workplace inflexibility issues.

The *Wall Street Journal* reported on April 11, 2012, in "Tire Makers' New Home," that Michelin decided to join Bridgestone Tire and Continental Tire in South Carolina with the building of a new $750 million manufacturing facility. The article noted that "Ohio, once the rubber capital of the world, now ranks as the 11th biggest North American tire producer...South Carolina, with daily production of 84,000 tires, today is second only to Oklahoma as the biggest tire producing state or province in North America." The North America president of Michelin noted that South Carolina "is also one of the least unionized states in the country, which gives the flexibility to focus on the customer. There is no significant difference between nonunion and unionized plants other than a rule book in our unionized plants that tell us what we can and can't do."

The mentality of the unionized workplace is one in which the position description drives activity. Going beyond it is not only frowned on by labor unions, but also actively litigated when employers request workers to go beyond the position description. So Honda Manufacturing in Marysville can use workers for varying purposes during slow times (i.e., post-Tsunami), while General Motors in Lordstown is strictly limited to legendary work rules running thousands of pages with strict job descriptions. The result: Honda is able to avoid layoffs and maintain higher productivity rates with its workers while General Motors has higher labor costs and lower productivity rates. The goal of this unionized rigidity is to require more workers and, therefore, more dues paying union members.

The same mentality is rampant in government. In our schools, the focus is on smaller classroom sizes despite the lack of data on its impact in student performance. In our cities, police and fire staffing levels are determined by national groups in order to drive up the number of employees needed. Our crime rates have dropped dramatically since 1990 and more than 75 percent of calls to fire houses involve non-structural fire issues, yet staffing increases.

For consumers over the last thirty years, this differential results in superior "foreign" cars being less expensive. In many cases, these foreign cars contain more American parts and labor than domestic cars. Growing up, my parents owned nothing but domestic cars. Today, my mom and all of my siblings drive cars made by Honda, Hyundai, Kia, or Mitsubishi. I've never owned any car other than a Honda. The same cost issue applies to commercial products across the gamut.

In government, labor unions use the system to enhance members at the expense of taxpayers. Ignazio Messina of the *Blade* reported on October 9, 2011, that the city had to pay overtime to a government worker who didn't work overtime simply because a co-worker pressed a button to prevent flooding in the city. It technically wasn't the job of the person who did press the button to press the button. It was the job of someone who was no longer at work. Because the actual button pusher didn't call the other worker and thereby prevented the other worker from getting overtime, the city had to pay the other employee four hours of overtime at time and a half his hourly pay rate for not working. Who cares that flooding likely would have occurred had the actual button pusher waited for the employee to make his way to the button? It wasn't about the city or taxpayers—it was about overtime pay for a union member. Messina noted that union members had filed a "staggering 3,115 grievances" against Toledo since 2001.

And then there is the role of labor unions in protecting employees who do wrong or do poorly. A week doesn't seem to pass without yet another report about a government worker or private sector union member engaging in conduct that is criminal or contrary to the best interest of his customers or employer. Anyone who has worked in a unionized environment has suffered from working with a co-worker who is lazy, inefficient, or deficient at his job. In those cases, the union usually does everything it can to protect these employees, including setting up "rubber rooms" where these employees spend their day doing nothing, but getting paid their full salaries.

Another point must be made on the issue of compensation differentials between workplace freedom states and forced unionization states. In "The Compensation Penalty of 'Right to Work' Laws," EPI found that workers in forced unionization states make roughly $1,500 more per year than workers in workplace freedom states. EPI attributes the pay differential to the presence of labor unions. The same study conceded that workplace freedom states had lower costs of living. Assuming the EPI finding is accurate, perhaps the differential comes from another element involving the freedom of workers—specifically, the legacy the institution of slavery had on the southern states that formed the Confederacy.

In 1853, the *New York Times* dispatched Frederick Law Olmstead, future architect of Central Park, to travel around the South and send back his observations. Olmstead wrote his dispatches from the South over the next two years. His columns later became a book titled, "The Cotton Kingdom: A Traveller's Observations on Cotton and Slavery in the American Slave States," first published 151 years ago in 1861.

Because Olmstead spent so much time in the South, staying in hotels and homes of southerners both rich and poor, and using the roads, rivers, and rails extensively, his observations provide a valuable snapshot in time. One of the most striking observations Olmstead made was the enormous economic and infrastructure difference between the northern manufacturing states and the southern agrarian states.

Of the North, Olmstead noted a traveler would find:

> A private room, where I could, in the first place, wash off the dust of the road, and make some changes of clothing before being admitted to a family apartment. This family room would be curtained and carpeted, and glowing softly with the light of sperm candles or a shaded lamp. When I entered it, I could expect that a couch or an arm-chair, and a fragrant cup of tea, with refined sugar, and wholesome bread of wheaten flour, leavened, would be offered me...I should expect, as a matter of course, a clean, sweet bed, where I could sleep alone and undisturbed, until possible in the morning a jug of hot water should be placed at my door.

On the South, Olmstead observed that a traveler would find:

Nine times out of ten...I slept in a room with others, in a bed which stank...I washed with utensils common to the whole household; I found no garden, no flowers, no fruit, no tea, no cream, no sugar, no bread...no curtains, no lifting windows...no couch—if one reclined in the family room it was on the bare floor-for there were no carpets or mats...the house swarmed with vermin.

In the South, "for nine-tenths of the citizens, comfortable homes, as the words would be understood by the mass of citizens of the North, are, under present arrangements, out of the question."

Without a doubt, the locus of economic freedom and prosperity in the 1850s resided in the manufacturing North. Recall it was to Ohio that the runaway slaves in Harriet Beecher Stowe's "Uncle Tom's Cabin, or Life Among the Lowly" so desperately tried to reach. In 1861, the North had twice as many people as the South. It had more than two times the miles of railroad track and nearly five times the number of factories. Those factories employed nearly ten times as many workers. The North produced more corn and had twice as many horses. Despite the weather advantage, the South, including Texas, only had 1.6 million more beef cattle than the North.

This concentration of economic power, enhanced by the devastation wrought in the South during the Civil War, would remain geographically fixed in the North for the next 100 years. Many states in the South maintained anti-freedom policies through the 1960s. Thus, the legacy of the institution of slavery cannot be dismissed when comparing economic conditions in the southern states.

For example, according to the Bureau of Economic Analysis, in 1930, which is nearly two decades before Congress passed the Taft-Hartley Act in 1947 allowing states to pass workplace freedom laws and before the height of labor union power, nine of the eleven confederate states had the lowest per capita personal income in America, with an average of only $309.93. In comparison, the fifteen states with the highest per capita personal income in 1930 had an average 155 percent higher ($789.87). Twelve of the fifteen top states were the northern states referenced by Olmstead.

By 2010, though some of the confederate states had matriculated up the chart (Virginia, Florida, and Texas), seven of the eleven still ended up in the bottom fifteen with an average of $33,328 in per capita personal income. The top fifteen states had an average of $45,790, which was 37 percent higher but much less than the difference in 1930. Nine of the fifteen top states still came from Olmstead's North.

Interestingly, the longitudinal results for Michigan and Ohio may show that the strength of labor unions hurts the long-term income of workers. In 1930, workers in Michigan and Ohio had the 13th and 12th highest per capita personal income, respectively. The automotive industry and other manufacturing facilities blossomed over the next fifty years, with heavy concentrations in those two states. As recently as 1970, Michigan and Ohio still held the 12th and 15th spots in per capita personal income. Yet, by 2010, the per capita personal income for workers in those states had slid to the 39th and 33rd highest in America. This slide corresponds to the rise of a globally competitive marketplace where the high cost and inflexibility of labor unions hinder states' abilities to adjust and compete with those market forces.

When comparing per capita personal income data controlling for the date when states enacted workplace freedom laws, the overall difference between workplace freedom states and forced unionization states shrinks as the years pass. In 1960, roughly ten years after the first set of states enacted workplace freedom laws, the difference in personal income between the two sets of states was 78.3 percent. Just a decade later, it had come down to just 16 percent. By 2010, the difference stood at 11.5 percent.

A final factor that must be considered when comparing compensation differentials between workplace freedom states and forced unionization states is the unsustainability of compensation paid in forced unionization states. Is it really accurate to cite inflated compensation advantages in forced unionization states, but ignore the compensation package realignments occurring at the companies responsible for those inflated compensation packages? The invisible hand of the market is what determines competitive compensation packages, and any company that ignores those market rates will either be forced to adjust or go out of business.

Three examples vividly illustrate this reality.

At both General Motors and Chrysler, workers received very generous compensation packages before the arrival of foreign cars hit the U.S. market. As foreign car makers introduced less expensive and more reliable cars, the domestic automakers lost market share and faced growing fiscal crises due to the overly generous compensation paid to workers—compensation that led to EPI's $1,500 premium in forced unionization states.

Both companies had to seek a massive bailout by the federal government. As part of the bailout, those companies have dramatically reduced the compensation of new workers. The companies have created a two-tier system where newer workers receive compensation substantially less than older workers doing the same work. The aim of creating the two-tier system was to become more competitive with the foreign carmakers in the workplace freedom states.

General Motors and Chrysler are in no way unique in putting in place two-tier contracts with labor unions. As the *Wall Street Journal* reported on May 29, 2012, in "Flat U.S. Wages Help Fuel Rebound in Manufacturing":

> With unemployment still high and global competition intense, employers have the upper hand in asking unions to relax work rules and restrain, or reduce, wages and benefits. Scores of U.S. companies have negotiated two-tier contracts with unions that allow them to pay new hires less than existing workers or otherwise restrain wage and benefit costs.

The article cites American Axle & Manufacturing Holdings Inc. in Michigan that is paying new hires $10.00 per hour for the same work legacy workers are getting $18.00 an hour to do. Another example given is General Electric Company's decision to relocate work back to Kentucky after the labor union agreed to a reduced starting hourly rate of $10.00, which is $8.00 to $10.00 lower than the old collective bargaining contract.

[JINO Alert #7: Media outlets should track and report on the realignment of compensation packages for private sector unions.]

The second example comes from Hostess Brands, Inc., the maker of Wonder Bread and Twinkies. Hostess recently filed bankruptcy because it could not compete with non-unionized baked goods companies. Hostess is seeking to reduce the compensation packages of workers so that it can stay in business. Hostess also is seeking to eliminate the other issue brought on by labor unions: workplace inflexibility.

Kyle Smith on February 15, 2012, at Forbes.com, noted that at Hostess, trucks going to the same location are prohibited from carrying both Wonder Bread and Twinkies. This practice increases the number of Teamsters, but adds a grossly inefficient cost to the bottom line. This inefficient practice is that once the two separate trucks arrive at the same destination, Hostess must employ two separate "pull-up" workers—one for bread and one for snacks—to unpack the trucks and place the goods in the store.

The third example focuses on the unsustainable defined benefit pension promises made mostly to unionized workers. The fact is that many companies simply cannot pay workers high salaries, contribute significant funds into defined benefit pension plans, and remain profitable or in business. According to Credit Suisse, a global financial institution, the private sector defined benefit pension deficit in the United States is $369 billion. Credit Suisse based its conclusion on analyzing the disclosures made by U.S. companies with defined benefit pension plans.

A final note on inflated union compensation. According to the Bureau of Labor Statistics, the median weekly earnings of union members was $923 in 2005 (adjusted to 2011 dollars). In 2011, the median weekly earnings of union members had only risen to $937, or just 1.5 percent in six years, which somewhat undermines Big Labor's dig that workplace freedom is really about the freedom to work for less. So much for the ability of labor unions to defy global competitive forces. What will be the argument for labor unions when the pay differential fades entirely?

Isn't It All About Jobs and Economic Growth?

As you mull over your big decision whether to make Ohio a workplace freedom or forced unionization state, here are other important facts you need to consider.

States that have decided to protect their workers' right to choose whether to join labor unions have experienced substantially more net job growth over the last two decades than states that force workers to join labor unions. According to the U.S. Bureau of Labor Statistics, from 1990 to 2012, states that protect workplace freedoms have averaged 38 percent net job growth compared to forced unionization states that have only averaged net job growth of 13 percent. That means workplace freedom states have added jobs at roughly three times the rate of forced unionization states since 1990.

During the same time period, of the fifteen states that had the highest net job growth, eleven (in bold), including the top six, protected the freedom of workers not to join labor unions. These states are **Nevada (83 percent)**, **Utah (81 percent)**, **North Dakota (73 percent)**, **Arizona, (69 percent)**, **Idaho (68 percent)**, **Texas (56 percent)**, Colorado (54 percent), Montana (53 percent), **Wyoming (52 percent)**, Alaska (52 percent), **South Dakota (50 percent)**, New Mexico (45 percent), **Florida (38 percent)**, the second most recent state to adopt workplace freedom legislation **Oklahoma (37 percent)**, and **Nebraska (35 percent)**.

Even states that suffered some of the largest job losses due to the massive housing construction declines (Nevada, Arizona, and Florida) still netted enormous job gains. Not surprisingly, except for Nevada (16.6 percent) the eleven workplace freedom states with the highest net job growth also have a unionization rate (the percentage of workers represented by labor unions) of ten percent or lower: Utah (7.1 percent), North Dakota (8.6 percent), Idaho (6.1 percent), Arizona (7.3 percent), Texas (6.3 percent), Wyoming (8.4 percent), South Dakota (6.5 percent), Florida (7.6 percent), Oklahoma (7.7 percent), and Nebraska (10 percent). Notably, of the four forced unionization states that made the top fifteen, all are located in the South or West of the United States.

In contrast, the fifteen states with the weakest job growth from 1990 to 2012 are all forced unionization states that form a rust belt from Missouri to Maine, plus California and Hawaii. These states are Connecticut (-3 percent), Rhode Island (0.8 percent), Michigan (3 percent), New Jersey (5 percent), Ohio (6 percent), Massachusetts (7 percent), New York (7 percent), Illinois (8 percent), Maine (10 percent), Pennsylvania (11 percent), Missouri (13 percent), Vermont (13 percent), California (14 percent), Hawaii (14 percent), and Indiana (14 percent). Indiana recently adopted workplace freedom legislation with the aim of breaking free from the northern pack of poorly performing job market states. As Indiana Governor Mitch Daniels acknowledged, protecting workplace freedom increases a state's competitiveness and stems the loss of companies and jobs that flee for more friendly environments.

Except in Indiana (12.4 percent) and Missouri (12.5 percent), the unionization rate in the worst performing states is above 13 percent: Connecticut (17.7 percent), Rhode Island (17.9 percent), Michigan (18.3 percent), New Jersey (16.8 percent), Ohio (14.7 percent), Massachusetts (15.4 percent), New York (26.1 percent), Illinois (17.2 percent), Maine (13.4 percent), Pennsylvania (15.8 percent), Vermont (13.5 percent), California (18.2 percent), and Hawaii (22.5 percent). In fact, more than half (8,425,000) of all workers represented by labor unions live in just seven states: California, New York, Illinois, Pennsylvania, Ohio, Michigan, and New Jersey—all among the worst job creating states in America.

In what may be the most jaw-dropping figure, despite possessing 65 million fewer people, workplace freedom states netted 11,806,400 jobs compared to forced unionization states that only added 7,873,200 jobs from 1990 to 2012. Fewer people, four million more jobs versus more people, four million fewer jobs is not a ringing endorsement of forced unionization or states like Ohio.

[JINO Alert #8: Media outlets should track and report on these jobs comparisons between forced unionization states and workplace freedom states.]

In terms of Ohio, it simply cannot be stated more clearly than this: Ohio's economy has been one of the worst in the United States over the last two decades. No matter what shorter time frame you analyze, Ohio is ranked among the weakest job markets in the country. From 38th best during the boom years of the 1990s to 50th best during the lost decade of the 2000s, Ohio's private sector netted a mere 245,600 jobs over the last 22 years, which translates to just over 11,000 jobs per year in the 7th most populous state in America.

Governor Kasich likes to claim that Ohio is one of the top private sector job producing markets in the country during his time in office. He likes to cite the raw number of private sector jobs added since January 2011, which is a bit misleading. In fairness to Governor Kasich, from January 2011 to April 2012, Ohio did add 78,100 private sector jobs, which is the 8th best in America. As the 7th largest state, Ohio should create more private sector jobs than most of the other, smaller states. As a point of comparison, during the last 15 months of Governor Strickland's term, Ohio's private sector added 68,300 jobs.

Not surprisingly, the states ahead of Ohio happen to be five of the six bigger states, with only hemorrhaging Illinois performing worse than Ohio. Both Michigan and Georgia, though smaller than Ohio, have added more private sector jobs than Ohio during Governor Kasich's term. A more accurate portrayal of private sector job growth is to rank the states by percentage change. Using that metric, Ohio falls to the 24th best private sector job market over the last 15 months. During that same span of time, Ohio had the 16th worst reduction in its labor market.

The pain is spread broadly across Ohio's industries. The fact is that there are fewer jobs today in Ohio than there were in January 1990 in four out of ten industry sectors: Mining & Logging; Construction; Manufacturing; and Information. In four other industry sectors, there are fewer jobs today than in January 2000: Trade, Transportation & Utility; Financial Activities; Leisure & Hospitality; and Other Services. The only two "healthy" industry sectors are Professional & Business Services and Education & Health Services, which can be attributed to that sector's dependence on government funding in K–12 education, higher education, Medicare, and Medicaid.

Ohio's private sector peaked way back in March 2000 with 4.85 million jobs. Even with the rosiest of assumptions, it likely will take another nine years or more to replace all of the jobs that have been lost.

Despite the sound bite offered by labor union zealots, the right to choose whether to join a labor union does not equate to the "right to work for less." Ask any Honda worker in Ohio if he or she works for less because Honda has remained union free since arriving in Ohio, or ask any Boeing worker in South Carolina working on the new 787 Dreamliner. Ask any new unionized General Motors or Ford worker in Ohio who now makes a lot less than his or her predecessor. It turns out that labor unions can't guarantee inflated wages against the tides of a globally competitive environment.

Workplace freedom states create more jobs and the growth of real personal income in those states exceeds the rate in forced unionization states. As Dr. Vedder found in the "Ohio Right-to-Work" report, from 1977 to 2008, the growth in real per capita income in workplace freedom states was 62.3 percent compared to just 52.8 percent in forced unionization states. Ohio fared even worse, experiencing just 35.7 percent growth in real per capita income.

Consistent with Dr. Vedder's report, in the last decade, as Ohioans experienced a per capita increase in personal income of 26 percent, workers in workplace freedom states saw their per capita personal income increase by 38 percent. This lower growth means Ohio families have less money in their pockets than they would have had if Ohio had protected workplace freedom over the last three decades. In 1900, Ohio's per capita personal income was 9.7 percent above the national average. Today, it is 9.4 percent below.

Using GDP as a barometer of economic growth, the workplace freedom states again outperform the forced unionization states. Over the last ten years, according to the Bureau of Economic Analysis, the increase in private sector GDP in workplace freedom states averaged 25 percent. The increases in private sector GDP in forced unionization states was eight points lower at 17 percent. Ohio, at -0.12 percent, had the 2nd worst percentage change in private sector GDP from 2000 to 2010. Only Michigan's -7.1 percent was worse.

Of the top 20 states that experienced the most private sector GDP growth, 13 were workplace freedom states. Of the 20 worst states, 15 were forced unionization states.

Narrowing the analysis to just growth in manufacturing GDP leads to similar results. Workplace freedom states averaged 26 percent as forced unionization states averaged 16 percent. The top 20 states included 13 workplace freedom states and the bottom 20 consisted of 15 forced unionization states. Ohio, at -17 percent, again came in 2nd from last just ahead of New Jersey's -24 percent. As detailed in "The Effect of State Policies on the Location of Manufacturing: Evidence from State Borders," by Thomas Holmes of the University of Minnesota and the Federal Reserve Bank of Minneapolis, "on average, the manufacturing share of total employment in a county increases by about one-third when one crosses the border into the pro-business [workplace freedom] side."

In terms of per capita real GDP growth from 1990 to 2010, workplace freedom states achieved 69 percent average growth versus 60 percent average growth in forced unionization states. Ohio came in even worse at 52 percent, leaving it with the 5th worst per capita real GDP growth over the last 20 years.

Finally, as private sector unionism has shrunk, the growth of labor union membership has exploded in government at every level. According to the U.S. Department of Labor, only 6.9 percent of private sector workers are members of labor unions. That is down from 33.9 percent at the peak of private sector unionism in 1945. In contrast, 37 percent of government workers are members of labor unions. That is up from 9.8 percent in 1945. Government workers are now 51 percent of all workers represented by labor unions. Such an outcome is odd given that of all types of employers, government is the one least expected to require labor unions to ensure it treats its workers well.

Along with the rise of public sector labor unions came the skyrocketing cost of government workers. The Congressional Budget Office reported in February 2012 that federal workers make significantly more than their peers in the private sector, regardless of education level. In fact, federal workers without high school degrees far out-earn their private sector peers. Despite this compensation package imbalance and the growing federal deficit, President Obama proposed giving federal workers pay increases in his 2013 President's Budget.

In terms of state workers, as noted in Chapter 4, "The Grand Bargain" report found that state workers received compensation packages worth 28 percent more than private sector workers. Governor Kasich just gave them an increase costing taxpayers $21 million per year.

A definitive study for local government workers is hard to do given the lack of transparency. What is clear from the school district fiscal data is that compensation packages for school employees are exceeding available tax revenues and outpacing inflation year after year. This escalation in compensation package costs is being placed on the backs of taxpayers, resulting in exploding property taxes.

According to the Bureau of Labor Statistics, in states that permit government workers to collectively bargain, the average yearly pay for state and local workers is $51,064 and $41,457, respectively. In contrast, in states that prohibit government workers from collectively bargaining, the average yearly pay for state and local workers is $46,025 (11 percent less) and $32,560 (27 percent less), respectively. If Ohio paid the 58,000 state workers on average $5,039 less, it would save taxpayers $292,262,000 per year. For local governments, the savings would be even bigger: $5,783,050,000 ($8,897 times 650,000 workers). Had Ohio's state and local governments kept pay in check, Ohio's state and local tax burden would have been smaller. At worst, there would not be the need for higher taxes.

Based upon the 2010 Annual Survey of Public Employment and Payroll by the U.S. Census Bureau, Ohio's state and local government workers received just under $2.5 billion in pay in March 2010. This monthly figure equates to roughly $30 billion in pay for the year. That amounts to a per capita tax of approximately $2,600 on every Ohioan. From 2000 to 2010, the average weekly pay increased by 37 percent for all state and local government workers. Some government workers had a phenomenal decade.

For example, the average weekly pay for hospital government workers went up by 73 percent. The average weekly pay for higher education support staff and professors increased by 56 percent and 54 percent, respectively. Firefighters average weekly pay jumped by 42 percent, and police officers experienced a 41 percent increase in pay. Public welfare workers also saw their average weekly pay rise by 41 percent. Keep in mind, those figures do not include any compensation package benefits except pay.

Now take a look at the migration data on where Ohioans moved to when they left Ohio. The migration data from 2000 to 2010 tells a provocative story. From 2009 to 2010, Ohio lost net residents to all but nine states. Of those nine states, the only workplace freedom states were Wyoming and Idaho. From 2000 to 2010, Ohio lost a net of 315,127 residents to other states. The total out migration over that period of time was 1.7 million residents. From 2009 to 2010, of the top ten states Ohio lost the most resident to, eight were workplace freedom states. In just one year, Ohio lost 22,310 net residents to workplace freedom states versus 8,715 net residents to forced unionization states. Over the decade, Ohio lost 245,039 net residents to workplace freedom states versus just 68,322 net residents to forced unionization states. These figures show that Ohio's policies and economic performance encourage citizens to vote with their feet in large numbers by moving to states that protect a worker's right to choose whether to join a labor union.

Whether it is job growth, personal income growth, gross domestic product growth, government cost increases, or migration data, states that protect workplace freedom are more attractive than states that protect labor unions.

The Right to Choose Is Fundamental to the American Way

The Constitution's First Amendment guarantees every American the right to freely associate with whomever they want and with whatever groups they want. The idea that Americans are forced to join labor unions as a condition of employment and forced to provide funds to labor unions that are used to promote values and ideas in direct conflict to their personal beliefs is wrong. All Americans should have the right to choose whether to associate with labor unions, and fear of losing a job or not getting a job should not be an issue in that decision.

Workplace freedom laws merely ensure that Americans are able to exercise that choice. Contrary to the claims of pro-union zealots, workplace freedom laws don't ban labor unions. They protect the right of workers to choose.

As reported in the *Parkersburg News and Sentinel*, the story of Jade Thompson illustrates the unfairness of the forced unionization environment. Ms. Thompson is a public school teacher in Marietta, Ohio. She is required to be a member of the Ohio Education Association (OEA). Her husband, Andy Thompson, was a Republican legislator. During the 2010 election, the OEA spent funds, a portion of which came from Ms. Thompson, to defeat her husband. One should never be forced to provide funds to be used against a spouse who is a candidate.

This type of forced contribution to causes and candidates that are contrary to the personal beliefs of members occurs across America every year. In 2011 in Ohio, thousands of teachers, police officers, fire fighters, and other government workers who supported the Senate Bill 5 reforms were forced to give money to the union political funds used to defeat the reforms.

All Ohioans deserve the right to choose.

So, What Would You Choose?

It is only from a very pro-union perspective that one can characterize the move to become a workplace freedom state as radical or right-wing. Why is the default position of federal law a pro-union position instead of a pro-freedom position? Why do states have to opt out of forced unionization rather than opt in to it? Even if pro-union forces provide a list of economic statistics to counter the data highlighted in this chapter, we are left with a debate in which both sides have supporting facts and data that help them make their cases.

Ohio needs to have the debate.

Instead of a robust debate, however, supporters of workplace freedom laws are called mentally retarded, anti-worker, anti-teacher, anti-police officer, and anti-firefighter. They are labeled as against the middle class. This type of school-yard name-calling masquerading as debate is unworthy of union organizers' heritage.

No wonder there is not a single worker freedom state wanting to become a forced unionization state. Not one of the now twenty-three states even considers it. Where is the underpaid, overworked coalition of citizens in those states demanding the enactment of a forced unionization law?

The labor movement won. The American workplace today is safer, cleaner, and more transparent than ever, and American workers are protected from arbitrary, capricious, and nefarious acts. Despite the presence of powerful labor unions from Missouri to Maine and California and Hawaii, labor unions are powerless to protect their members from the shocks of a globally competitive marketplace and from the advance of technological innovations that reduce the need for workers.

Labor union bosses can complain about free trade and cheap labor in places like China and India, but they cannot force companies to maintain expensive and inflexible operations in the United States. Labor union honchos cannot force companies to be profitable. Companies that cannot make profits, will disappear.

It is far better to have strong job growth rather than strong labor unions.

To enact a workplace freedom law or make any significant reforms, it is critical to understand the political landscape in Ohio.

Otherwise, reform efforts will not succeed.

9

WHAT COLOR IS OHIO?

"Republicans can't win the presidency without winning Ohio."

Understanding Ohio's political landscape takes a lot more than spending a day in reputed bell-weather Chillicothe, Ohio, once every four years. The path to the White House goes through the Electoral College where each state gets a set number of electoral votes (the number of congressional seats) to cast for the popular vote winner. That means basic math drives the race to get the magic 270 Electoral College votes required to win.

The path to the White House is much more difficult for Republicans. This difficulty is due to the populations of red versus blue states that form the base for each party. It is safe to say that by the 2000 election, the political realignment geographically was nearly complete. This realignment resulted in the New England, Rust Belt, and Pacific states reliably voting blue, with the Rocky Mountain, Southwest, and Southern states voting red.

There are exceptions, of course, and those exceptions are the battleground states. Ohio is one of those exceptions.

Regardless of the nominees, based on results over the last three decades, 46 states and the District of Columbia can be assigned already. President Barack Obama likely will win the following states: California, Connecticut, the District of Columbia, Delaware, Hawaii, Illinois, Maine, Maryland, Massachusetts, Michigan, Minnesota, New Jersey, New York, Oregon, Pennsylvania, Rhode Island, Vermont, Washington, and Wisconsin.

Governor Scott Walker's recall victory in June 2012 provided some indications that Wisconsin may be in play in 2012, but despite their best efforts, Republicans haven't won Oregon, Washington, or Wisconsin since Ronald Reagan's 1984 landslide win. Bush's 1988 win was the last one for Republicans in Illinois, Michigan, and Pennsylvania. Republicans haven't won Minnesota since Richard Nixon in 1972. Thus, President Obama or any Democrat enters the election with a blue base of 242 electoral votes.

Former Massachusetts Governor Mitt Romney likely will win states worth 180 electoral votes: Alabama, Alaska, Arizona, Arkansas, Georgia, Idaho, Kansas, Kentucky, Louisiana, Mississippi, Missouri, Montana, Nebraska, North Dakota, Oklahoma, South Carolina, South Dakota, Tennessee, Texas, Utah, West Virginia, and Wyoming. All but West Virginia are reliably Republican, and President Obama's job-killing moves against coal render him done there.

Given the Republicans' downfall with the financial crisis in September 2008 and then Senator Obama's "blank slate" with voters, his wins in Indiana, North Carolina, and Virginia likely won't be repeated. Voters know him now, and he won't have better conditions than he did in 2008. Those three Republican states likely will return to historical form, giving Republicans 219 electoral votes.

Based on this preview, Democrats today typically begin the general election with an advantage of 23 electoral votes. The remaining battleground states are mostly small players with fewer than ten electoral votes. These battleground states dot the landscape from coast to coast.

New Mexico (5 electoral votes) is the toughest call, but President Obama's sizable win in 2008 portends a repeat in 2012. In 2008, he won Colorado (9) and Nevada (6) by 9 and 12.5 percentage points, respectively. Senate Majority Leader Harry Reid of Nevada and Senator Michael Bennett of Colorado both survived the 2010 Republican wave. Coloradans also elected a Democrat governor who remains very popular. The likelihood that President Obama will lose either state is thus low, leaving him with 262 electoral votes.

With those allocations, President Obama is a mere eight electoral votes shy of reelection with only 57 electoral votes remaining in Florida (29), Iowa (6), New Hampshire (4), and Ohio (18). Although he won Iowa by 9.5 percent in 2008, the state tossed out the Democratic incumbent and put a Republican in the governor's office in 2010.

New Hampshire strongly supported President Obama in 2008, but cut Democratic Governor John Lynch's win from 41.3 percent to just 7.6 percent in 2010.

In Florida, President Obama's stance toward Israel has hurt him with Jewish voters. Governor Romney may add Senator Marco Rubio to the ticket to secure Florida.

President Obama won Ohio in 2008 by 4.5 percent, but it went heavily Republican in 2010. As discussed in Chapter 6, the Republican attempt to curb public sector unions in 2011 backfired when unions engineered a huge popular vote defeat of the legislation in November 2011. This exercise gave Democrats a trial run for 2012.

Republican primary turnout in these states in 2012 was weak, indicating a lack of enthusiasm for Governor Romney.

President Obama can win reelection by taking Florida, Ohio, or both Iowa and New Hampshire. In contrast, Governor Romney must win Florida and Ohio and either Iowa or New Hampshire to win.

This path presents a narrow opportunity to win the presidency and allows for few errors. This precarious path is not unique to the 2012 election. A look back at the 2000 and 2004 elections show that, for Republicans, victory only comes by winning Florida and Ohio. In 2000, Bush picked up Colorado, Nevada, and New Hampshire, but lost Iowa and New Mexico. To get to 271 electoral votes, Bush had to win both Florida and Ohio. In 2004, Bush lost New Hampshire, but won Colorado, Iowa, Nevada, and New Mexico. Without Florida and Ohio, however, he could not have secured the 286 electoral vote victory.

Keep in mind, over the last five presidential elections, the Republican candidate has won twice and only by one and sixteen electoral votes, respectively. The winning Democratic candidates have won by 100, 109, and 192 electoral votes. The last large Republican presidential victory occurred in 1988 when George H.W. Bush won what many people believe was President Reagan's third term.

With the 2010 Census results, the population shift to red states has improved the electoral map for Republicans, but not enough to make Florida and Ohio states that Republicans can afford to lose. As the popular saying goes, no candidate has won the White House without winning Ohio since John F. Kennedy in 1960 and no Republican has won the White House without winning Ohio period.

It goes without saying that if the economic data continues to be negative, especially in terms of job growth, the above state allocations could change dramatically. If the United States follows European countries into a double-dip recession, then President Obama's chances dim considerably. It would be mildly ironic if President Obama loses due to an economic crisis given that his election in 2008 largely occurred because of the negative impact the economic crisis in September 2008 had on the Republican brand.

So what is unique about Ohio that makes it such a vital battleground state?

Big Blue Cities and Red Rural Counties Reflect National Mood

The issue facing Republicans in Ohio is the same issue facing Republicans nationally with the Electoral College: we are losing too many big "blue" counties (or "blue" states) by too large a margin, thereby forcing us into a very low margin of error strategy. Specifically, if the Republican statewide candidate loses the eight counties with the largest cities in Ohio by the margins won by Governor Strickland in 2006 or President Obama in 2008, then that candidate must win the remaining counties by fairly large margins, which, at best, would result in a razor thin win.

Ohio has eight large counties that provide the Democratic candidate a large margin of votes (defined as 15,000 votes or more). These counties are Cuyahoga, Franklin, Lorain, Lucas, Mahoning, Montgomery, Summit, and Trumbull. The cities in these counties are Akron, Cleveland, Columbus, Dayton, Lorain, Toledo, and Youngstown. Over the last three presidential elections, these counties have provided Democratic margins of victory of 140,731, 259,842, and

507,317. In the last two heavily contested gubernatorial races, those counties provided the Democratic candidate with margins of victory of 612,800 and 116,840.

On their side, Republicans only have four counties that consistently provide margins of victory in excess of 15,000 votes. Those counties are Butler, Clermont, Delaware, and Warren, which are the three counties surrounding Hamilton County in southwest Ohio and the county just north of Franklin County in Central Ohio. As the population in Cincinnati has moved out of Hamilton County into Butler, Clermont, and Warren counties, Hamilton County obviously has become less red with margins ranging from roughly 30,000 for President Obama in 2008 to just over 11,000 for Governor Kasich in 2010.

Of all the votes cast for the two major candidates in Ohio over the last five presidential elections, 41 percent came from the eight big Democratic counties. The Democratic candidates garnered almost 26 percent of all votes cast in Ohio in just those eight counties. Because of this reality, the Democrats can win Ohio by grabbing large margins of victory in those eight counties and holding their own in the remaining 80 counties. Mathematically, there comes a point at which the margin of victory in the eight counties is too large for the Republicans to make it up in the remaining counties.

Based on a detailed analysis of each county, any Democratic candidate who can win the 12 big Democratic and Republican counties by 400,000 votes will win the election because there are not enough votes in the remaining smaller counties to erase this lead. Doing so would require winning a 56 percent margin in the remaining 76 counties. Keep in mind, in addition to the eight big Democratic counties, there are another 14 counties that are reliably blue—meaning, those counties provide Democrats with wins averaging less than 15,000 votes per election. Thus, the playing field for Republicans really consists of 62 counties.

For example, in 2008, Senator John McCain won 66 counties compared to 22 counties for President Obama, yet Senator McCain still lost by over 260,000 votes. President Obama exited the big eight counties with a half million vote lead. Those eight counties accounted for 2,350,016 votes out of the 5,617,864 votes cast for the two major party candidates, which meant Senator McCain would have needed to win the remaining votes by a 58 percent margin to squeak out a one vote win.

Many people incorrectly believe that the 2004 campaign in Ohio represents the blueprint for success. In 2004, the Republicans placed a gay marriage amendment on the ballot with the belief that it would drive conservative turnout and secure a victory for Bush. The turnout did indeed jump from 63.90 percent to 71.77 percent. The problem, however, is that the votes cast for Democrat Senator John Kerry increased by more than 25 percent, as the votes cast for President Bush only increased by 21.6 percent. Senator Kerry won the 12 counties by almost 260,000 votes. Thus, President Bush's 2004 victory in Ohio was nearly 47,000 votes narrower than his 2000 victory when he lost the popular vote nationally.

A more detailed analysis shows just how poorly President Bush performed in 2004 compared to then Governor Bush in 2000. In thirteen counties, President Bush did better than the Republican statewide average from 1998 to 2004. In those counties, President Bush only gained 18,592 more votes than Governor Bush. There was little change in four other counties. In 71 counties, President Bush did worse than (5.4 percent less) the Republican statewide average from 1998 to 2004. In 19 counties, President Bush performed more than 8 percent below the Republican statewide average from 1998 to 2004. He lost 166,979 votes from 2000 to 2004 in those counties.

In 2006, Governor Strickland rode a Democratic wave based on anti-Bush sentiment and years of Republican scandals involving Governor Taft and Tom Noe in Ohio. Governor Strickland's 62 percent win over Secretary of State Ken Blackwell was unprecedented for a Democratic candidate. Governor Strickland's margin of victory in the eight counties totaled more than 613,000 votes. That wave swept Democrats into all but one statewide office, including a U.S. Senate seat, and gave them control of the Ohio House.

How historic was Governor Strickland's victory? He ran up the largest non-presidential vote total in 87 out of 88 counties. In fact, his 2006 vote total was just 11 percent below Senator Kerry's 2004 vote total. Despite the higher voter turnout in presidential year elections, Governor Strickland actually received more votes than Senator Kerry did in 2004 in 63 of 88 counties. He holds the highest vote total for a Democratic gubernatorial candidate in all 88 counties.

Two years later, with Bush's presidency ending on the sour note of the September financial meltdown, President Obama won the election and Ohio. President Obama won by 507,000 votes in the 12 key counties, which made it impossible for Senator McCain, a moderate, to make up ground in Ohio's conservative rural counties. This outcome was foreshadowed during the 2008 primary when Senator McCain and/or his message failed to gain traction in 31 key Republican counties.

Despite being the *de facto* nominee with 918 delegates in hand by the time the Ohio primary vote occurred (Governor Romney was the next closest with 286 delegates), Senator McCain received less than 55 percent of the votes in top Republican counties. Senator McCain did best in the Greater Cleveland area and in Democratic counties where his moderate views held more sway. The more conservative Governor Mike Huckabee picked up more than 30 percent of the total primary vote. Senator McCain's lackluster performance with conservative Ohioans crushed his ability to win Ohio in the general election.

President Obama and the Democrats, however, misread the results of the elections in 2006 and 2008, believing that America and Ohio had become center-left entities. The results in 2010 squashed that belief. Just like Governor Strickland and President Obama, Republicans rode an anti-Obama wave in 2010. With the economy still floundering despite President Obama's two years in office and Governor Strickland's four years in office, Ohioans gave Republicans total control of government. With victories in all statewide offices and a return of control in the Ohio House, Republicans were positioned to enact major reforms to fix Ohio.

Unfortunately, like President Obama, Governor Kasich misread the outcome as a vote for <u>him</u> rather than a vote <u>against</u> President Obama and Governor Strickland. As other statewide Democratic candidates lost by large margins, Ohioans nearly reelected Governor Strickland, which evidenced voter concern with Kasich. Governor Strickland lost by less than 80,000 votes, largely due to low turnout in the eight Democratic counties and strong turnout in the four Republican counties. Governor Strickland's 613,000 vote margin in 2006 shrank to an 117,000 margin in 2010.

This schizophrenic pattern makes predicting the 2012 outcome incredibly difficult. Will the big eight Democratic counties turn out in margins like 2006 and 2008? Will Governor Romney suffer the same fate as Senator McCain? The key to winning Ohio is to understand that a Republican candidate's odds of winning increase as the conservative base is energized. Even though translating primary election results to general election results is fraught with pitfalls, the 2012 Republican primary results don't bode well for winning in November.

No matter how you slice it, the news out of Ohio on Super Tuesday was simply not good.

Governor Romney and his team could not hide his continued inability to get a majority (versus a plurality) of the vote in a contested battleground state. Governor Romney has been running for the presidency for more than five years, and he barely won. He won only 19 of Ohio's 88 counties—eight of which are Democratic counties. In 47 of the 69 counties that Senator Santorum won (68 percent), Governor Romney garnered roughly the same or fewer votes than Governor Huckabee did in 2008 when the primary race didn't matter in Ohio. Governor Romney's poor performance occurred despite grossly outspending his weak primary opponents, which won't work against a well-funded President Obama.

Even a review of counties where Governor Romney won shows the problems he had in Ohio. Contrary to Governor Romney supporters who cite his wins in the Democratic and southwestern corner counties as proof that he will be competitive in key President Obama counties and drive up margins in key Republican counties, the data just doesn't support that conclusion. In Cuyahoga County, with 33 percent more primary voters than in 2008, Governor Romney earned roughly 6,000 fewer votes than Senator McCain. In contrast, Senator Santorum more than doubled Governor Huckabee's vote total, and Speaker Newt Gingrich nearly matched it. This means the other, more conservative candidates actually increased the vote total in the Cleveland area, not Governor Romney.

In Franklin County, with 9,000 more votes cast than in 2008, while Senator Santorum improved upon Governor Huckabee's second place showing by grabbing 12,000 more votes, Governor Romney lost over 17,000 votes that Senator McCain received. In Montgomery County, as Senator Santorum received 1,300 fewer votes than Governor Huckabee, Governor Romney got 8,000 fewer votes than Senator McCain. In Stark County, Senator Santorum's 1,000 vote increase over Governor Huckabee occurred as Governor Romney earned 9,000 fewer than Senator McCain. In Summit County, Senator Santorum's 4,000 vote jump over Governor Huckabee is less than Governor Romney's 6,000 vote decline from Senator McCain.

In the southwestern corner of Ohio, even though Governor Romney won all five counties, the results are less than meets the eye. In Hamilton County, the votes cast for the Republican candidates declined from 2008 to 2012 by roughly 2,000 votes. Even though Senator Santorum earned 5,000 more votes than Governor Huckabee, Governor Romney won with 15,000 fewer votes than Senator McCain. In Butler County, Senator Santorum lost ground to Governor Huckabee by 1,000 votes, but Governor Romney lost even more ground to Senator McCain by over 7,000 votes. In Clermont County, Senator Santorum's 1,200 vote increase from Governor Huckabee is far less than Governor Romney's 5,000 reduction from Senator McCain's vote total. In Greene and Warren counties, as Senator

Santorum received roughly the same number of votes as Governor Huckabee, Governor Romney earned 2,500 and 3,400 fewer votes than Senator McCain did in 2008, respectively. Just like the Democratic counties, the votes Governor Romney lost compared to Senator McCain that Senator Santorum didn't win, went to other candidates. This outcome foreshadows an uphill battle for Governor Romney in November.

Taking a step back from the particular candidates, the low voter turnout in Ohio also signals serious trouble for Republicans in November. The projected final Republican vote count was only about 6 percent higher than the 2008 total when the Ohio primary largely didn't matter and, equally troubling, was more than 1.1 million votes less than the total cast in the Democratic primary in 2008. Acknowledging, of course, that anything can happen between now and November—remember the September 2008 financial meltdown, the low voter turnout indicates a continued lack of enthusiasm by the conservative base, thereby making an Ohio win in November highly unlikely.

Because President Obama will run-up large margins in the blue urban Ohio counties (the ones Governor Romney won), Governor Romney, as President Bush did in 2004 and Senator McCain did not do in 2008, must grab as many votes from the conservative red counties as possible (the ones Governor Romney lost). For all the pundit talk about appealing to the middle, since 1976, Republicans lost when their presidential candidate was a moderate and won when he was a conservative: President Reagan won in 1980, 1984, and 1988 (his third term won by then vice president Bush) and President Bush won in 2000 and 2004 while President Gerald Ford lost in 1976, President

Bush lost in 1992, Senator Bob Dole lost in 1996, and Senator McCain lost in 2008. Winning independents does little good when your base abandons you. It appears the conservative base does not support Governor Romney.

Predictive Tools

As part of a data analysis tool, I created two models in 2008 that proved highly accurate in predicting the outcome of the 2010 gubernatorial race. The first model focused on producing specific vote targets in 64 Republican counties, 18 Democratic counties, and six toss-up counties. This model projected a razor thin victory by Kasich of 16,619 votes, which was roughly 60,000 votes off the actual result. That difference between the actual outcome and the predicted outcome represented less than two percent of all votes cast.

The second model focused on margins of victory and/or defeat in 33 key counties. The targeted margin of victory in 25 counties and the targeted margin of defeat in eight counties were determined based on several streams of data. Hitting the targets would allow the Republican candidate to enter the remaining fifty-five counties down just 68,500 votes. This model projected a Kasich win between 31,500 votes and 100,000 votes. The midway point was 65,750, or just 12,000 or so votes off the actual result.

These tools were used to issue vote predictions on the eve of the 2008 presidential election. On Monday, November 3, 2008, using the data analysis tools, I made specific vote projections by county on Senator McCain's expected margins of victory or defeat in his race against President Obama. For this project, I ignored the votes of the other candidates, as none of them had any impact on the outcome of the election. Those projections were made entirely based upon a county-by-county analysis of data. It should be noted that polling companies only make statewide percentage projections, as county-by-county vote total projections are much more difficult and expensive to make, as doing so would require large sample sizes in each county compared to a statewide sample size.

Based on the results, my projections were within 2 percent or less of the actual results in forty-eight counties (55 percent). In another eighteen counties, the projections were within 2.01 percent and 3.5 percent of the actual results, which means that the projections were within a typical poll margin of error in 75 percent of Ohio's counties.

The RealClearPolitics final polling average statewide predicted a 2.5 percent margin of victory for President Obama, which was within 2.1 percent of the actual final result of 4.6 percent. RealClearPolitics averages the public results from the various polling companies it considers legitimate. The statewide margin of defeat projection for Senator McCain predicted a possible loss by 20,345 votes. His final vote deficit was 262,224 votes, which was 2.15 percent more than the projection. Given that the projections were made without the benefit of any internal polling data, the excellent results from the predictions confirm the underlying soundness of the data analysis tool.

This chapter started with the quip that understanding Ohio took more than spending a day in bell-weather Chillicothe every election cycle. Chillicothe may be a good predictor, but, as part of the analysis of each county, I identified counties that proved highly accurate at reflecting the winner in statewide races. I refer to these counties as "mirror" counties. Some of these counties did far better than Chillicothe at predicting winners and with votes far in excess of the votes cast in Chillicothe.

From 1998 to 2010 and across 28 races, two counties voted for the winner in every race. With between 75,000 and 120,000 votes to cast depending on the type of election, Lake County sits in northeast Ohio along Lake Erie with roughly 230,000 people. Mentor is the largest city in Lake County. According to the Census Bureau, in 2010, Lake County was mostly white (95 percent) with 56 percent of households comprised of married couples. The median age of the county was 39 years old and the median household income was $48,763.

Sandusky County possesses between 18,000 and 29,000 votes each election cycle. It also touches Lake Erie, but in the northwest side of Ohio. With roughly 60,000 people, Sandusky County was 92 percent white with Fremont serving as the largest city. Like Lake County, 56 percent of households held married couples and the median age and household income in the county were 37 and $40,584, respectively.

In another seven counties, the voters correctly picked the winner in 27 out of 28 races. I refer to these counties as "near mirror" counties. The seven counties are Carroll, Huron, Medina, Ottawa, Richland, Seneca, and Wood. Three of these counties voted for the loser of the 2008 presidential election by a total of just 2,218 votes (Carroll County by 674 votes, Huron County by 808 votes, and Seneca County by 736 votes).

Lastly, six more counties accurately predicted the winner in 26 out of 28 races, or 95 percent of the time. The "close mirror" counties are Clark, Coshocton, Guernsey, Marion, Morgan, and Muskingum. Interestingly, four of these counties (Coshocton County, Marion

County, Morgan County, and Muskingum County) incorrectly picked Betty Montgomery in 2006 as the Attorney General winner. Within two years, the actual winner, Marc Dann, had resigned from office in disgrace and under a cloud of corruption. Clark County missed the correct 2000 presidential winner by just 324 votes and the 2008 presidential winner by 1,676 votes.

All told, the 15 counties that accurately pick the winner of Ohio statewide races 95 percent or more of the time cast over 620,000 votes in the 2008 presidential election and 400,000 votes in the 2010 gubernatorial election, which represented 11 percent of all votes cast in those elections. Anecdotally, all 15 counties voted "No" on the Senate Bill 5 veto referendum in 2011. Polling data from those counties would appear to be the most reliable data for candidates and the results on election night are almost all but certain to predict the winner.

For politicians and strategists looking to get elected or to enact major reforms on issues such as workplace freedom, government pensions, and state and local taxes, understanding the color of Ohio is vital to winning. This data must be translated into a broad strategy that details the plan for winning. As highlighted in Chapter 6, the Republicans who led the government collective bargaining reforms contained in Senate Bill 5 failed to put a strategy in place before moving forward on the legislation.

The strategy to win any big reform effort in Ohio must start out with a firm understanding of Ohio's political landscape and layout a pathway to victory that takes into account the potential vote disadvantage in the big blue counties.

10

WHAT TO DO ABOUT IT: SEVEN REFORMS NEEDED TO
FIX OHIO

President Ronald Reagan: "Raising a banner of no pale pastels, but
bold colors."

The problems facing Ohio are detailed throughout this book. Given the data, no reasonable person can look back on the last 40 years and conclude that Ohio's elected officials have consistently made the right decisions about our state's economy. Ohio has gone from being an economic leader to being an economic laggard. Our economic position is well below the national average. Our job market is creating fewer private sector jobs. State and local government spending exploded, thereby requiring a heavy tax burden that makes our state a less attractive place to live and work.

Ohio's current malaise centers on three broad problems. First, our political system doesn't work. This leads to timid actions for fear of losing power or to a tendency to focus on the wrong problems. Second, state and local governments spend too much money. This is partially due to the power of government labor unions driving compensation package costs beyond the ability of taxpayers to pay without a burdensome tax load. Third, Ohio's economy remains mired in an outdated and inefficient model that undervalues workplace freedom and flexibility.

Let's look at the bigger picture. In January 1990, Ohio had 4,126,900 private sector (non-farm, non-government) jobs. Florida had 4,520,400 private sector jobs. By January 2012, Ohio had 4,363,600 private sector jobs, an increase of 236,700 jobs in 22 years. That works out to 10,759 net private sector jobs per year, or a net increase of just 5.7 percent.

In contrast, Florida currently has 6,208,300 private sector jobs, an increase of 1,687,900 jobs since 1990. That translates to 76,723 net private sector jobs per year—even after the horrible housing and construction losses over the last three years. Florida's net private sector job growth is up 37 percent from 1990. That means Florida netted on average 6.5 times more private sector jobs than Ohio each year over the last 22 years. Florida now has 42 percent more private sector jobs than Ohio, up from 9.5 percent more in 1990.

Ohio hit its peak number of private sector jobs way back in March 2000 when it had 4.85 million jobs. Florida's private sector jobs peaked at 6.96 million jobs in March 2007. Currently both states are down roughly 11 percent from their peaks.

Florida does have a higher unemployment rate, but it also created substantially more jobs since January 1990. Florida went from just 393,500 more private sector workers than Ohio in 1990 to 1,844,700 more private sector workers today. Florida's higher unemployment rate has more to do with the fact that a lot more people have moved to Florida over the last two decades. An influx of people means that a recession likely will result in higher unemployment. Ohio was home to 10.864 million people in 1990. By 2010, Ohio's population had grown by 6.2 percent to 11.536 million.

In stark contrast, Florida didn't surpass Ohio's population total until late in 1983 and was home to 13.033 million people by 1990. That figure exploded by more than 44 percent over the next twenty years, reaching 18.801 million in 2010.

Florida isn't the only state to beat Ohio over the last 22 years. When comparing the jobs in each state using Ohio's private sector job count in January 1990 and January 2012 (meaning, how many jobs each state had at those times using Ohio's job tally as the constant), only Rhode Island (-.5 percent), New Jersey (-.8 percent), Michigan (-2.4 percent), and Connecticut (-2.8 percent) performed worse than Ohio. Forty-five states closed (had a lower rate in 1990 but improved by 2012) or increased the gap (had a higher rate in 1990 and widened the margin even more by 2012) between jobs possessed in 1990 compared to Ohio and jobs possessed in 2012 compared to Ohio.

In addition to Florida, of the 16 other states that increased (versus closed the gap) their private sector job record compared to Ohio, 11 of the states give workers the choice whether to join labor unions. From Texas at 66 percent to Louisiana at 6.1 percent, Ohio and the majority of forced unionization states didn't keep pace over the last 22 years.

Of course, Ohio will add jobs as the economy expands, just like it did in the 1990s. The issue isn't whether Ohio will add jobs. It will. Rather, the issue will be the pace of the expansion, especially compared to other states.

The reforms outlined below all focus on placing more power in the hands of Ohioans and less power in the hands of politicians, political parties, government entities, and labor unions. The reforms would significantly increase the transparency of government entities and the accountability of government to the people.

Key Reform #1: Free Ohio Workers and Companies by Making Ohio a Workplace Freedom State

We must fundamentally reform Ohio's job market to make it more competitive in today's global environment. If Ohio wants to accelerate job creation and significantly increase its competitiveness, it must move to protect the economic freedom of workers who choose not to join labor unions and to free employers from the rigidity of costly and burdensome labor contracts.

Ohioans for Workplace Freedom has launched a signature drive to place a ballot initiative before voters. Given the data in support of workplace freedom, Ohioans should get the right to vote on this critical issue. If you agree this is important, you can contact Ohioans for Workplace Freedom (www.ohioansforworkplacefreedom.com) to find out how you can make this vote happen.

Once enough signatures have been gathered and submitted, the ballot issue will be placed on the following November election ballot. If the fight over Senate Bill 5 proved anything, it is that the labor unions will spend whatever it takes to preserve the status quo and their power. The labor unions likely will exceed the $42 million that they raised to defeat Senate Bill 5 to kill workplace freedom reform.

If grassroots Ohioans and the business community fail to financially support the passage of a workplace freedom law, it will not pass. Period. This ballot issue will be the last chance Ohio's economy has of escaping the outdated economic model that prevents it from becoming a jobs leader. The results in Wisconsin show that labor unions can be defeated.

The global marketplace has made it harder than ever to maintain a competitive edge. If Ohio wants to increase its competitiveness and win its share of jobs in the future, it must make it easier for its citizens and their employers to keep costs down. An economy with more freedom will spur entrepreneurship and innovation and provide Ohioans a path to increased prosperity.

ACTION: Volunteer to gather signatures for Ohioans for Workplace Freedom and work hard to pass the ballot initiative.

Key Reform #2: Change the Political System by Returning Power to the People

It is important to fight with the establishment and politicians to maintain term limits. Term limits have not entirely solved the problems with Ohio's dysfunctional political system, but it curtailed the rise of lifelong legislators. As the saying goes, absolute power corrupts absolutely.

Plus, no politician is so uniquely gifted that she needs to spend an entire career in the state legislature. In fact, we must get past the notion that politicians are somehow so special that they are irreplaceable. They are not.

We should appreciate our legislators' public service and their willingness to serve, but we must never let them forget that they serve us. They also must focus on the job we send them to the legislature to perform. Term limits force them to focus on getting the important things done.

We should, however, reform the political system to empower the grassroots. Having returned to Ohio in 2007 after nine years in Colorado and Washington, D.C., I've watched how the political parties dominate the system. Whether it is the active endorsement of candidates in a primary or the appointment process used to fill vacancies, a handful of Ohio party bosses have too much power. The recent fight between Governor Kasich and former Republican Party Chairman Kevin DeWine over control of the Ohio Republican Party illustrates this power problem.

My own experience in a highly competitive district where the grassroots held the power is much more consistent with American democracy. In 2002, I left the practice of law to run a congressional campaign in a newly drawn district in Colorado. The district had a registration split in thirds by Republicans, Democrats, and unaffiliated voters.

Because of the system and the neutrality requirement, the Republican primary drew five candidates: Bob Beauprez, an owner of a $300 million bank and the Republican State Party Chairman; Joe Rogers, the sitting Lieutenant Governor; Sam Zakhem, a former state legislator and ambassador to Bahrain under President Reagan; Mark Baisley, a dot-com millionaire; and, my candidate, Rick O'Donnell, the governor's 32 year-old policy director who had no campaign experience. It was clear from the beginning that the establishment wanted Beauprez to be the candidate. In fact, he received endorsements from the entire federal delegation except Senator Wayne Allard who stayed neutral and Representative Tom Tancredo who endorsed O'Donnell.

We knew O'Donnell had to win the assembly, which is the key way candidates get on the primary ballot, in order to have any chance for him to win the primary. An assembly win would raise doubts about Beauprez's candidacy and give O'Donnell the chance to raise the money necessary to win the primary. The other candidates had assets

O'Donnell lacked: Beauprez and Baisley were millionaires, and thus could self-fund; Zakhem and Rogers had name identification from past elections and thus could appeal to voters; Rogers also had the lieutenant governor's title to help him raise funds. Our game plan was to own the grassroots, which Colorado's system allows candidates without money to do.

From the caucus to the assembly, O'Donnell and I worked the delegates zealously. We attended every breakfast, lunch, dinner, or other event held by Republican or center-right groups in the district to make our case. By the night of the assembly, Baisley had dropped out of the race and both Zakhem and Rogers had decided to gather signatures to get on the primary ballot. It was going to be an assembly fight between Beauprez and O'Donnell—the establishment versus the grassroots—David versus Goliath.

Our plan for the assembly was simple: in words and visuals, we strove to create a stark contrast with Beauprez that convinced delegates that O'Donnell had the ability to win. Our pre-assembly scouting of the location allowed us to create that contrast from the moment the delegates arrived. With limited nearby parking, we knew many older delegates and delegates with kids would have to walk a fair distance in the heat to get to the building, so we rented several extra long golf carts, adorned them in campaign material, and had volunteers zip delegates from their cars to the building. We also secured the only meeting room where we played videos of President Reagan and provided delegates with food and cold bottled water with our labels attached.

Bill Armstrong, the former U.S. Senator and top conservative in Colorado, nominated Beauprez. Senator Armstrong did a great job, as usual. Beauprez then stood behind the podium and gave his speech from the raised stage. Beauprez did a good job, as his voice had the familiar sound of the Motel 6 commercial narrator and his biography is a classic American story.

To contrast O'Donnell with Beauprez, we had three delegates from the district nominate O'Donnell (Senator Armstrong didn't live in the district), including his mother. We had secured ahead of time the only wireless microphone at the facility, which gave O'Donnell the ability to deliver his speech without the podium. As an extra little piece of contrast, because O'Donnell also was a delegate (Beauprez was not because he had moved into the district just to run for the seat), we had him carefully come down the stairs of the stage as he was speaking to show he was one of them—of the grassroots. O'Donnell gave a phenomenal speech that made the case for his candidacy.

To the shock of the establishment and the media, O'Donnell won the assembly. One long-time media figure, Peter Blake, commented in his June 1, 2002 column in the *Rocky Mountain News*:

> O'Donnell's exuberant handlers are convinced these little touches helped their 32-year-old candidate take top line on the Aug. 13 primary ballot at the 7th Congressional District GOP assembly Thursday night. He defeated the better-known, better-funded Bob Beauprez, the former state GOP chairman, by a margin of 50.5 percent to 45 percent.
>
> Oh, and the fact O'Donnell drove to the doors of the 165 delegates he couldn't reach by phone and talked to them in person or, if they weren't home, left a signed note.
>
> Not that Beauprez was depressed. Manager Sean Murphy maintains they did pretty well considering that O'Donnell had been campaigning longer.

For the past month the candidates have devoted themselves exclusively to the pre-assembly, 382-delegate universe. But now they must reach the general primary voter, and Beauprez's money might turn the tide. The field will be broader, since former ambassador Sam Zakhem and Lt. Gov. Joe Rogers are likely to make the ballot by petition.

The 7th District GOP assembly might have been the last, and greatest, hurrah for the caucus-assembly system and its personal-touch politics.

It was an incredible night for the grassroots in Colorado.

We engaged in a massive grassroots volunteer effort that allowed us to knock on thousands of primary voter doors and, with a little money that O'Donnell had saved up, send a few direct mail pieces to primary voters. We had no money for radio or television. Beauprez, after writing his campaign a $450,000 check, put ads on radio and television the last two weeks of the primary. On the morning of the primary, both our polling and Beauprez's polling had us winning.

After the voting ended, the results showed that we had crushed both Zakhem and Rogers. As for Beauprez, after outspending us 5-1, he beat O'Donnell by 1,959 votes. After the primary, Dick Wadhams asked me to help him get Senator Allard reelected. Wadhams was a legend in Colorado politics and had been involved in some of the biggest races during his career. I jumped at the chance to learn from one of the best in the country in one of the top five races in the country. Dick would go on to help John Thune defeat Senator Tom Daschle.

As for O'Donnell, he went to work to help Beauprez win the general election in a very competitive district. Beauprez won by just 121 votes. He would unequivocally tell you that O'Donnell's stiff primary challenge made him a better candidate and helped him win one of the top races in the country.

My own experience in Colorado and experiences thereafter have engrained in me a few lessons that I think could improve Ohio's political system. Those lessons are (1) competitive districts are good for the political system, (2) the political system should empower the grassroots, (3) forcing political parties to be neutral during the primary promotes competition, and (4) party neutrality doesn't necessarily mean that the establishment won't try to select the winner in other ways. The reforms listed below embody these lessons.

A. Competitive Districts Are Good for the Political System

First, eliminate the gerrymandering of congressional and state legislative districts and draw those districts with two key goals in mind: preserving communities of interest (such as keeping a city within one district) and making the districts as competitive as possible (an equal number of registered Republican, Democratic, and unaffiliated voters). While in the short run it might be appealing to gerrymander districts to create as many safe partisan seats as possible, in the long run, what is gained by gerrymandering also is lost by gerrymandering when the political pendulum swings the other way, which it invariably does.

The focus on registration equity versus outcome equity is simple. Creating new districts based upon outcomes assumes that recent past performance indicates future performance. Advocates of outcome equity really are trying to obtain certain results. Our Founding Fathers required a census every ten years to escape the passions of the moment. They also altered the election of Senators as compared to Representatives to ensure one body wasn't driven by current events.

This approach ignores the external factors that often drive elections.

For example, the historic Democratic wins in 2006 had far less to do with the actual candidates and far more to do with voter disgust with Republicans. If we drew legislative districts based upon those results, then we would not have very competitive districts.

Drawing legislative districts using registration data ensures that districts would be competitive from a voter standpoint. Specifically, in most cases, registered Republicans vote for Republicans, registered Democrats vote for Democrats, and unaffiliated voters vote for the left or the right. In all three groups, a small number, however, do vote differently from election to election. These voters are the ones who decide elections.

Obviously, it is mathematically impossible to draw all 132 state legislative seats with an equal number of Republican, Democratic, and unaffiliated voters without absurdly violating communities of interest. The goal should be to draw as many legislative seats as competitively as possible. We don't need every seat to be competitive to increase accountability, we just need enough seat to be competitive to threaten control of the legislature each cycle.

Proponents of competitive districts not only have the more principled position, but also a more effective practical tool. With competitive districts, incumbents will focus more attention on serving their constituents knowing that their next election is anything but guaranteed. When a majority of districts lack any real competitive element, the politicians can ignore the people. If we want more accountability, then we need to force all politicians to truly compete in each election for our support.

ACTION: Pass legislation or a ballot initiative requiring competitive legislative districts.

B. The Political System Should Empower the Grassroots and Force Political Parties To Be Neutral During the Primary to Promote Competition

Competitive primaries are a good thing. Proverbs teaches us, "As iron sharpens iron, so one man sharpens another." In Colorado, candidates have two routes to gain access to the primary ballot. The main route is by earning 30 percent or more of the delegate votes at the specific assembly. The candidate who secures the most delegates at the assembly earns the top-line listing on the primary ballot. If a candidate fails to secure 30 percent of the delegate votes, but more than 10 percent, then that candidate is permitted to gather a requisite number of signatures to qualify for the primary ballot. If a candidate fails to get 10 percent of the delegate votes at the assembly, that candidate is ineligible for the primary ballot.

A second route is to skip the assembly and secure the requisite number of signatures to gain access to the primary ballot.

By adopting Colorado's caucus-assembly-primary model, grassroots Ohioans in both political parties would gain power. First, delegates to the assemblies are selected at the precinct caucuses, so candidates must work the grassroots to get their delegates to attend and earn a spot on the assembly delegate list. This reform should increase citizen participation in Ohio and strengthen the grassroots.

Next, candidates then have to convince the grassroots delegates to the assembly of their candidacy in order to gain enough votes to make it to the primary. Once the precinct caucus delegate results are public, candidates must spend time visiting with the delegates to earn their support. This process allows candidates to demonstrate their skills and also allows delegates to winnow the field by measuring candidates in an up close and personal manner.

Finally, at the assembly, candidates each get a chance to address the delegates to make one final push to earn their support. Once the speeches are over, the delegates vote. Because earning the top-line designation is so important, candidates put enormous effort into winning the assembly. Other than time, this part of the process is not unduly expensive, so even candidates with little personal resources are able to compete. Money doesn't necessarily drive the outcome of the process.

Once the assembly ends, the primary begins with all of the candidates who either earned enough delegate votes at the assembly or who gathered enough signatures. Money matters a lot more during the primary, as getting on radio and television may drive the outcome.

In conjunction with moving to a Colorado caucus-assembly-primary model, political parties should be neutral throughout the primary process. The system in Ohio today that places endorsement power in the hands of political parties makes it all but impossible for non-endorsed candidates to win. With the endorsement comes the money to win the primary and the expectation that the winner will show loyalty to the party when in office. That loyalty rides roughshod over the interests of the people who live in the winner's district.

Why should a handful of party bosses possess the power to choose who wins a primary? Wouldn't it be better if the people in the district possessed the power to choose who represented the party in the general election? Wouldn't it improve constituent service if incumbents knew that they might have a primary opponent and had to defeat that opponent mano-a-mano without party support?

Ohio needs candidates and politicians who are not tied so closely with the political parties. This reform would open the political system to those men and women who haven't spent their lives serving the parties. With a political system more accessible to Joe or Jane Ohioan, perhaps we'd get better results out of the legislature.

ACTION: Pass a ballot initiative to adopt the Colorado caucus-assembly-primary model and require neutrality by the political parties in primaries.

C. Party Neutrality Doesn't Necessarily Mean That the Establishment Won't Try to Select the Winner in Other Ways

Most of the activities supported by groups such as the Koch brothers, Karl Rove, and other 527 or PAC groups use the bulk of their resources on federal issues and federal candidates. Those groups are also top-down entities led from outside Ohio. I don't have any problem with their work or focuses. That said, there are too few groups that focus on state candidates and issues on a consistent basis.

If we really want to win, we must have a robust candidate recruitment and training system. We know that the existing crop of politicians will break their promises or will refuse to enact the big reforms. To ensure accountability and keep the pressure on them to do the right thing, we must identify and train credible candidates who can run in primaries and win.

Because party neutrality does not necessarily mean that the establishment won't do what it can to make sure its candidates win, conservatives should launch an entity that identifies conservative candidates and then helps them via independent activities to win office. This entity would allow conservative candidates who may or may not also get support from the establishment to wage competitive primary and general election campaigns.

This entity, which I will refer to as the Ohio Conservatives Fund, should be modeled after Senator Jim DeMint's Senate Conservatives

Fund. As its website states:

> [The Senate Conservatives Fund] is a grassroots organization dedicated to electing strong conservative leaders to the United States Senate. We do not support liberal Republicans and we are not affiliated with the Republican Party or any of its campaign committees. SCF seeks to bring bold conservative leadership to Washington by supporting candidates who have the courage to fight for the timeless conservative principles of limited government, strong national defense, and traditional family values.

The Ohio Conservatives Fund should have a similar mission, but focus on Ohio legislative and state offices.

Importantly, the establishment or the typical people who serve the establishment must not control the Ohio Conservatives Fund, as such control would defeat the entire purpose of the entity. This entity must be run by grassroots individuals who identify themselves primarily as conservatives and secondarily as Republicans.

This entity also should strategically fight tax increases at the local level, including targeting elected officials who support those tax increases. The goal of engaging in local elections is to counter the funding of labor unions and vendors, thereby serving as a defender of taxpayers. By targeting key jurisdictions and winning, this group can have a chilling effect on efforts to continually raise taxes on Ohioans.

ACTION: Create a non-establishment campaign fund to identify and promote conservative candidates and fight local tax increases.

Key Reform #3: Replace the Second Legislative Session With Oversight & Sunset Functions

Currently, Ohio's General Assembly operates for two years divided into two sessions. The sessions run from January to June, with other activities occurring during the remainder of the year. Legislators introduce proposed legislation during both sessions. Committees first consider the legislation and hear testimony for, against, or about the legislation from interested parties. If successfully passed out of the committees, the entire body in which the legislation was first offered debates and votes on it. The legislation then goes through the same process in the other body. If also passed by the other body, assuming no changes were made, the legislation is presented to the governor for his signature or veto.

After 209 years, are there really that many issues facing Ohio requiring a legislative fix? Is it not possible that providing legislators with two sessions to introduce and pass legislation opens the door to lots of needless nibbling? If legislators are spending the bulk of their time on proposed new laws, what other actions aren't being done that might make Ohio government more efficient and effective?

Ohio does not need a legislature that meets and passes legislation every year. The core legislative function of passing laws should be reserved for the first session of a two-year assembly. This reform would force the legislature to do a far better job using its finite resources to hold hearings and debates on <u>necessary</u> legislation. The urgency created by this change would increase the seriousness of proposed laws and amendments.

Conversely, Ohio does need a legislature that performs a more rigorous oversight and sunset function. The work done by the Inspector General and the audit functions performed by the State Auditor are important, but both entities lack the resources to truly review all legislatively created programs. The legislature should spend the second session of each assembly conducting oversight hearings on all state government programs, including sunset reviews.

The primary focus of the legislature should be to determine if every government program satisfies the following requirements:

- Does the program have performance metrics that can be used to determine effectiveness?
- Does the program do what the legislature intended it to do?
- Under a cost-benefit analysis, do the program's benefits outweigh its costs?
- Does the program perform functions that overlap with other programs and, if so, does consolidation of those programs make economic and programmatic sense?
- Are there productivity gains that could be made by reforming the program?
- From a sunset review standpoint, should the program be reauthorized?

This oversight and sunset review function would allow the legislature to make more informed decisions on spending and would force government program managers to demonstrate the continued need and efficacy of their programs.

Every government program should be analyzed and put through a sunset review every eight years. The legislature should issue reports on programs detailing their activities and the justifications for their actions.

For taxpayers, this process and the information generated by it would significantly increase the transparency of state government and the accountability of both government programs and the legislature. State government would no longer be operated largely on autopilot.

ACTION: Pass a ballot initiative instituting the above changes.

Key Reform #4: Reform How Government Works

Ohio's government entities are in dire need of reforms that focus on making those entities more efficient and effective. From increasing worker productivity to eliminating burdensome regulations to identifying areas to institute spending cuts, Ohio's state and local governments can and should do a better job as stewards of finite and precious taxpayer dollars. Below are several recommendations that can fundamentally change how Ohio works.

Legislators should pass true government pension reforms. Real reforms as outlined in both Buckeye Institute reports "The Grand Bargain" and "Hanging by a Thread" would ensure taxpayers would not be on the hook for a bailout. These reforms include the following: a shift to a defined contribution system like Michigan did in 1997 or a shift to a true hybrid system like Democratic-led Rhode Island did in 2011, using career salary averages without add-ins such as overtime to determine the pension, and reducing the COLA to the Social Security COLA. Such reforms, however, also would significantly lower the pensions of government retirees, including politicians, to reflect those retirements common in the private sector in Ohio.

With the proliferation of websites and widespread access to the Internet, workers today have many distractions that lessen their productivity at work. As reported in the *Enquirer*, many private sector companies are putting in place restrictions on Internet access or the websites that can be reached on work computers. The *Enquirer* report highlighted that "more than 50,000 YouTube videos were being downloaded from company computers every day" at Procter & Gamble.

As I noted in testimony submitted to the Ohio House Legislative Study Committee on Technology on September 20, 2011:

> One of the last vestiges of the American workplace
> lacking in measurable productivity gains is government.
> Although computers have improved workplace
> productivity, computers also can lead to a decrease in
> productivity. With the widespread adoption of

computers with Internet access and spotty blocking policies across state agencies, a more thorough auditing of IT usage on behalf of state employees is warranted.

We all know that at some level or another, workers are going to occasionally visit Facebook, ESPN.com, or other non-work related websites. Unlike private sector workplaces, however, the state has a responsibility to the taxpayers to ensure that tax dollars are being used as efficiently and effectively as possible...

As the Deputy Director of the Colorado Department of Regulatory Agencies under Governor Bill Owens, we conducted a limited, two-week audit of state employees and discovered that a majority of audited workers were spending more than 20 percent of their day—some as high as 60 percent of their day—on non-government related websites. This audit occurred in 2003—well before the mass use of Facebook, YouTube, and other popular websites.

This abuse of government computers isn't unique. The most famous recent case occurred at the U.S. Securities and Exchange Commission when 17 senior employees spent hours a day looking at pornography instead of doing their jobs as regulators. This abuse occurred as the U.S. financial system collapsed.

Many state and local governments don't use software to block access to non-work related websites. Government entities that do use website blocking software don't deploy it comprehensively or do so only selectively. For example, at her request, I met with Ohio Secretary of State Jennifer Brunner to hear about her effort to make government social service and health data accessible via her website. Because part of her effort looked a lot like the Buckeye Institute's Better Days Ohio county economic data tool, I tried to load the Buckeye Institute website. It wouldn't load. It turned out that someone in Secretary

Brunner's office had blocked the Buckeye Institute website on the Secretary of State's server.

To prevent abuse and increase productivity, all state and local government entities in Ohio should block access on government computers to the top 1,000 websites visited by workers that have no relation to their government functions. With less time spent surfing the Internet, government worker productivity should increase markedly. After all, what is good for private sector productivity also should be good for government sector productivity.

It also is high time to eliminate prevailing wage requirements from government-funded projects. This requirement unnecessarily drives the cost of public projects up by 10 percent to 30 percent, which requires a higher tax burden.

Ohio also must create a more accountable system to reduce unemployment and workers compensation abuse. During conversations with business leaders in seven counties across Ohio, I was surprised to hear that the number one problem that businesses face is finding qualified workers who will accept job offers. These leaders repeatedly told me that they would offer a job to a candidate who would turn down the job because that individual made more or, after factoring in gasoline, child care, and other costs, made nearly as much on unemployment. Many candidates interview just to fulfill the paperwork requirement to get unemployment compensation.

Ohio quickly should create an easy-to-use, online reporting system that allows employers to notify the Ohio Department of Jobs & Family Services of job offers made to individuals that were declined. That information then can be used to cutoff unemployment compensation. With Ohio already owing the federal government over

$1.8 billion in loans from the Federal Unemployment Trust Fund, we must eliminate fraud from the system. No Ohioan who rejects a job offer should be able to game the system and have their poor choices subsidized by other Ohioans.

Regulatory requirement also must be reduced. As one business leader I talked to said, "We pay a lot of scorekeepers" referring to the army of accountants, lawyers, compliance staff, and consultants required to keep ahead of regulatory requirements. Those professions may benefit, but such overhead costs undermine the growth of Ohio companies and slow job creation. Too often, business leaders interact with government bureaucrats more interested in being adversaries than strategic partners.

According to business leaders, Ohio has too many forms, too many rules, and too many processes. Although Lieutenant Governor Mary Taylor has done a commendable job with the Common Sense Initiative program, that concept needs to be put on steroids and a top-to-bottom review of all state government regulations must be conducted.

The Institute for Justice recently released its "License to Work: A National Study of Burdens from Occupational Licensing" report containing the 2012 rankings of the states. The Institute for Justice ranked Ohio as the 12th "most broadly and onerously licensed state." The report ranked Ohio low due to "exceptionally high barriers compared to the other states" and because "some of Ohio's licensure requirements also appear excessive compared to those of other occupations licensed by the state." As I noted in my March 17, 2010 critique of Governor Kasich's state budget, "It also would have been reassuring to see one regulatory body eliminated to demonstrate

Governor Kasich's view that Ohio needs fewer, not more, regulations." Instead of eliminating regulatory bodies, Ohio has added new ones to its list.

A big problem highlighted by business leaders across Ohio is the responsiveness and inconsistent enforcement of building codes. Business leaders cited conflicts between building plan examiners and building inspectors. Businesses reported losing significant amounts of money due purely to delays. A similar complaint focused on the inconsistencies between the Ohio EPA and the federal EPA in inspecting and approving activities. Businesses and farmers should not be subject to the lottery of "depends on who you call" when it comes to running their businesses.

On higher education reform, Texas Governor Rick Perry challenged public higher education in Texas to educate students for $10,000 or less. With more taxpayer funds being directed to research, he demanded greater transparency on productivity of faculty members regarding teaching loads and research activities. Admirably, Governor Perry wants to find the true financial returns Texans receive for investing in public higher education.

Due to the relentless pursuit of the faculty productivity data by Rick O'Donnell (the same O'Donnell whose Colorado congressional campaign I ran in 2002), Texans discovered that their precious taxes and tuition payments are being wasted at the University of Texas and Texas A&M. O'Donnell highlighted four key findings in his groundbreaking report, "Higher Education's Faculty Productivity Gap: The Cost to Students, Parents & Taxpayers":

- Students and taxpayers are charged hundreds of millions of dollars more than necessary to subsidize low productivity;
- Top scholars who bring in almost all the research funding see

large amounts of their grants siphoned off to pay for the overhead of their less productive colleagues;

- Thousands of students are deprived of opportunities to learn from the most senior faculty members, raising troubling questions about quality; and,
- The faculty who do the most teaching perform under working conditions that make them second or third class citizens, with low-pay, few benefits and little, if any, job security.

O'Donnell came up with five classifications for faculty members: (1) all-around Stars (high teaching loads and high externally funded research dollars); (2) adjunct Sherpas (high teaching loads, but low externally funded research dollars); (3) research-focused Pioneers (low teaching loads, but high externally funded research dollars); (4) tenured and seniority-protected Coasters (low teaching loads and low externally funded research dollars); and (5), within Coasters, a subclass of Dodgers (low teaching loads, low externally funded research dollars, but high per student costs).

With higher education being one of the largest state budget items and with ever-exploding tuition fees, O'Donnell's framework should be applied to all faculty members at Ohio four-year and two-year public higher education institutions to identify how to reduce costs and provide greater value to students by dealing with the latter two groups. With the U.S. Department of Education recently ranking four of Ohio's public four-year colleges in the top 14 most expensive public colleges (Miami University #2, The Ohio State University #10, Ohio University #13, and University of Cincinnati #14), this analysis is needed immediately to help bring down the cost for Ohioans to attend public colleges.

Another aspect that must be thoroughly analyzed is the bloat in public higher education related to both programs and courses. As noted in the "Six Principles for Fixing Ohio" report, Ohio has too many publicly-funded law schools that are among the lowest ranked in the country and has too many similar undergraduate course offerings that drive taxpayer costs up. Ohio must reduce the number of programs offered and invest more resources in the better programs to keep those programs among the best in America.

By leveraging technology, Ohio's top professors can teach online courses to all interested students at all colleges and universities, thereby providing more students unique learning experiences and reducing the number of professors (and their lucrative pensions) and costly physical space needed to teach the same course at a dozen or more locations. If Stanford and Harvard can do it, so can Ohio State, Cincinnati, and Akron. With higher education student loan debt topping $1 trillion, we must do more in Ohio to bring down the cost and improve the quality.

Business leaders also complain about the bias in government in funding higher education over the traditional trade schools and technical colleges. A four-year degree is a great asset to have, but for many Ohioans, it just isn't likely to make sense given the financial costs incurred to get the degree and the opportunity cost spent sitting in a classroom. For those Ohioans, a stronger two-year and trade school system would allow them to gain valuable skills that could be used to fill the high-skill jobs needed by Ohio companies.

ACTION: Run candidates in primaries against politicians who fail to push for these government reforms.

Key Reform #5: Reduce State and Local Government Spending and Enact Broad State and Local Tax Reform

This reform is fairly simple: stop spending so darn much money.

Whether it is the 148 percent increase in state general revenue fund expenditures from 1990 to 2013 or the 33 percent jump in school district expenditures in ten years, state and local governments across Ohio spend too much money. We just can't take it anymore.

Accounting for population growth and inflation, the state general revenue fund expenditure budget should be around $22 billion instead of $27 billion. Governor Kasich and the legislature should take a microscope to the state budget and find roughly $6 billion to cut. Other than a lack of political will, there is no reason why our elected officials can't realign the state budget to reflect a more reasonable growth curve.

As for local governments, had per pupil expenditures tracked inflation and student growth over the last decade, Ohioans would have paid $2.1 billion less in taxes.

Ohio cannot expect to become a leader among the states carrying one of the highest state and local tax burdens. For too many years, politicians have enacted tax policies while ignoring the impact such policies have on other government taxes. The long-term outcome over time is that the net state and local tax burden on Ohioans gets bigger and bigger.

According to the Tax Foundation, in 1977, Ohio's state and local tax burden was the 40th highest in America. By 2005, it had risen to the 5th highest in America. With the commercial activity tax reform in 2006 under Governor Taft, Ohio's state and local tax burden improved to the 18th highest by 2009. With the economic slowdown, the likelihood that Ohio's state and local tax burden improved in 2010 and 2011 is unlikely.

As noted previously, Ohio's state income tax is in the middle of the pack. It is Ohio's local tax burden that drives the overall state and local tax burden into the top twenty among the states. As a vivid demonstration of the local tax burden, the Federation of Tax Administrators (FTA) reports in its "2009 State & Local Source Revenue" report that Ohioans pay $65.4 billion in state and local taxes, with 53.8 percent coming from state taxes and 46.2 percent coming from local taxes. Of the 13 states with a higher percentage of taxes coming from local taxes, seven are states with no state income tax or a flat state income tax. The other six include high tax states such as California and New York.

Excluding corporate income taxes, according to the FTA, a higher percentage of Ohio tax revenue comes from local property taxes (29.8 percent) than from state and local income taxes (28.7 percent). Yet, politicians focus almost exclusively on reducing state income taxes and ignore what is happening to local property taxes. The state income tax generates roughly one-third of all state-level taxes.

Enacting a comprehensive tax reform package that covers state and local taxes is critical to ending the burden shifting from state taxes to local taxes. With property taxes being the primary source of local taxes, solving the education funding dilemma is critical. That means clamping down on education expenditures.

First, Ohioans already provide generous funding to school districts. According to the Ohio Department of Taxation, from 2001 to 2010, property taxes charged statewide increased by 31.8 percent. At the same time, the value of property only went up by 20.3 percent. Property taxes in 2001 totaled 5.7 percent of property value. By 2010, that figure had risen to 6.2 percent. Though seemingly small, the difference equates to $1.35 billion. Thus, the property tax burden on

Ohioans is increasing at a much faster pace than value of the property being taxed.

As with all federal, state, and local government spending, we must move toward a model that substantially increases cost transparency. By cost transparency, I mean the true cost to the individual (or household) of a government program. Public K-12 school districts have three pipelines of funding: local funding via property and school income taxes (and bonds), state funding, and federal funding. Because of these three distinct pipelines, school district residents really have no idea how much they actually pay to support their local schools. This same lack of true cost transparency exists for other local governments, as well.

In fact, because of these funding pipelines, most Ohioans understate how much it costs to run their local governments. The general view is that the cost is reflected in local property and/or income taxes. This grossly understates the true cost and therefore limits transparency and accountability.

For example, in 2010-2011, Dublin City Schools, a wealthy suburb, received $127,071,386 from local property taxes and $34,130,776 from state taxes, which represented 76 percent and 20 percent of all revenue, respectively (the remaining 4 percent came from federal taxes). Most Dublin residents likely don't factor in the portion of their state taxes that gets sent back to Dublin City Schools. This bifurcated pipeline conceals the true cost of running schools.

Setting aside the issue of federal funding for a moment (see the next solution), if Ohioans had to fund 100 percent of the costs of their school districts locally, they likely would demand greater cost controls and spending accountability from school district administrators. For some Ohioans, their state taxes subsidize school district costs in other locations, including in affluent locations that have the resources to cover their own costs.

More money is simply not the answer. Equality doesn't mean that every Ohio student should have the exact same amount of money spent on him. If a wealthy community wants to invest a greater level of resources into its school district, then those taxpayers should have the right to tax themselves to do so. That higher spending shouldn't, therefore, translate into higher spending everywhere else. Far more important than the amount of money spent is that each school district has the minimum amount of funds to provide every Ohio student with a basic education.

In fact, using the 2010-2011 education data, the median per pupil expenditure of Ohio's school districts was $9,566. That figure, however, is inflated. From 2001 to 2011, school district expenditures went up 33 percent, yet those school districts are educating 6 percent fewer kids today. After adjusting for pupil shrinkage and inflation, the median per pupil figure should be $8,505.

If every Ohio student cost $8,505 to educate, Ohio's school districts would spend roughly $13.9 billion per year versus the $17.5 billion those entities spent in 2011. This figure is well below the actual revenues collected by Ohio's school districts, which totaled $17.3 billion. Ohio taxes used to fund the schools could be lowered by $3.4 billion. You will notice that the actual expenditures compared to actual revenues left us with a $200 million statewide deficit in 2011.

The bottom line is that had school districts controlled expenditures, Ohio taxes would be lower even after providing additional support to poor school districts to ensure every Ohio child receives a basic level of education funding. With school districts in areas with the resources covering 100 percent of school funding through local means, higher cost transparency would result in far stronger accountability and, most likely, slower expenditure growth.

Before any tax reform is enacted, however, two other reforms must occur. First, school districts and other government entities should be required to realign compensation packages to better reflect inflation, demographics, and the economic reality of Ohio's private sector. Homeowners across the state have lost significant value in their homes, yet school districts want higher taxes. This disconnect must be eliminated.

Consider these facts: for the 609 school districts for which there is data, expenditures outpaced inflation in 440 school districts. In nearly half (287) of the school districts, expenditures exceeded inflation by more than 10 percent and in 136 cases more than doubled inflation. If expenditures are adjusted to reflect both inflation and student increases or decreases, 546 school districts had expenditures in 2010 that surpassed inflation, with 408 school districts outpacing inflation by 10 percent or more and 169 school districts exceeding inflation by at least two times as much.

Ohioans deserve greater transparency into the negotiations that occur between government managers and government labor unions. One way to do this is to publicly release the various offers made by each side during the collective bargaining process. One innovative school district in Ohio deserves enormous praise for voluntarily doing this. The Brecksville-Broadview Heights City School District began posting the proposals on its "Negotiations News" website (http://www.bbhcsd.org/negotiations/) to increase the transparency for school district residents. This action will allow taxpayers to follow and to track the negotiations and get involved if the proposals don't keep a lid on compensation package costs.

Secondly, there must be some consolidation of government entities. Ohio does not need and cannot afford to fund over 3,700 local government entities. As highlighted in the November 2011 Buckeye Institute report "Joining Forces: Consolidation Will Help Ohio's Local Governments If Compensation Package Costs Are Properly Managed," four of the five school districts in Marion County easily could be consolidated, which would save taxpayers roughly $2 million per year. As the "Joining Forces" report notes, consolidation does not mean closing schools, losing mascots, or losing historical connections in our communities; rather, consolidation means eliminating many administrative positions, streamlining busing operations, and leveraging assets more effectively.

Once compensation packages are realigned, consolidation occurs, and true cost transparency is realized, the frequency and size of future tax increases must be reduced. To limit the frequency, local government entities, including school districts, should be restricted to running levy increases only during general elections in November. This reform ensures that local government tax increase requests are decided when the most number of eligible voters turn out to vote. It also prevents local governments from coming back to voters during primary or special elections immediately upon losing, thereby requiring local government leaders to reevaluate the requests.

To limit the amount of tax increases, the level of transparency must increase so voters easily can educate themselves on the fiscal decisions made by local governments. Local governments should be required to submit several pieces of data for publication on the State Auditor's website. The format of this data should allow easy comparisons between the percentage increases and inflation, as too often government entities are providing yearly compensation package increases that outpace inflation year after year. That practice guarantees that taxes will have to go up to cover these significant cost increases.

The first piece of data is the total yearly cost of <u>each</u> benefit in every collective bargaining agreement entered into with a government labor union, including the percentage increase of each cost compared to the current year expenditures. The second piece of data is the total yearly cost of compensation packages for all employees, including the percentage increase of those costs compared to current year expenditures. The final piece of data is the total yearly cost and percentage increase from the previous year of each compensation package benefit provided to non-unionized employees, including elected officials, part-time employees, and administrators.

As evidenced by the above analysis regarding school district property taxes, there is significant room for reforms in Ohio. As urged in the "Six Principles for Fixing Ohio" report, Governor Kasich should convene a multi-day tax summit involving leaders from all state and local government entities to create a real tax reform agenda that will drive Ohio's overall state and local tax burden down, making it more competitive with other states.

ACTION 1: Governor Kasich should host a statewide tax reform summit with representatives from all government entities to develop a plan to lower the total tax burden on Ohioans.

ACTION 2: Run candidates in primaries against politicians who fail to support these reforms to rein in spending and reduce taxes

at the state and local levels.

Key Reform #6: Take Power Back from Washington, D.C.

The federal government is bankrupt financially and intellectually. It simply cannot continue to nationalize issues and programs. When our country was created under the U.S. Constitution, the Founding Fathers created a tripartite sovereignty system. This system is embodied in the 10th Amendment.

Beginning in the New Deal era, the federal government's role expanded due to judicial findings under the Commerce Clause and Necessary and Proper Clause that enabled the federal government to involve itself in more aspects of our lives. As the federal government's powers grew, the powers of state and local governments shrank. The justification for this one-size-fits-all approach rested on the inefficiencies resulting from different state standards and on the alleged "race to the bottom" that would occur if the federal government didn't restrict the states ability to set standards.

Beyond the serious constitutional defects of this approach, of which there are several, more practically, the one-size-fits-all approach undermines the powerful force implicit in the principle of federalism that the 50 states should compete with each other on policies and approaches. This competition, rather than resulting in a race to the bottom, would incent political leaders to provide taxpayers with the best goods and services at the lowest cost. With the mobility of Americans in the 21st century, politicians would work hard to keep their citizens from moving to better functioning states.

Moreover, the increase in transparency that came with the technological birth of smart phones; the rise of 24-hour news channels; the adoption of social media tools like YouTube, Twitter, and

Facebook; and the growth of permanent oppositions from political parties, bloggers, and other quasi-political entities substantially reduces the risk of a race to the bottom. This transparency drives greater accountability, as no politician wants his poor decisions or "race to the bottom" impacts on vulnerable populations amplified by smart phone videos on YouTube, cable television news, blogs, tweets, or Facebook posts.

It is more than past due to have a national dialogue on decentralizing powers back to state and local governments. Governor Kasich should attempt to lead this national conversation to restore the states' primary role on issues such as education, energy, Medicaid, and transportation. Ohio taxpayers should not be forced to subsidize other states, nor should other states be forced to subsidize Ohio, which is what nationalization of programs functionally does.

For example, as the *Dispatch* reported on February 20, 2012, in "Donor State: While Ohio's roads crumble, the state must send hundreds of millions in gas-tax money to Washington to help fix roads in other states," Ohioans subsidized transportation infrastructure in other states with $1.5 billion of our tax dollars over the last decade and over $5 billion since 1956. By states providing subsidies to other states, the current system eliminates the connection between state governments' costs and taxpayers. As noted in Key Reform #5, we need more true government cost transparency so that taxpayers fully understand the costs of programs and can make educated decisions on those programs.

Not only should power over programs return to the states, but the tax revenue also should stay in the states. Rather than engage in block grants, tax transfers, or other federally-controlled maneuvers, federal taxes should be cut to reflect the total cost of the programs returned to the states. This federal tax reduction will allow each state to raise state income taxes to directly fund the programs, thereby increasing real tax competition among the states.

No more will citizens of one state be forced to subsidize the domestic policy decisions of other states. Equally important, states will no longer be incented to provide goods or services they can't self-fund or to delay reforming their programs. As part of implementing this competitive federalism idea, federal taxes should be cut by the amount spent on the programs to be decentralized. Governors and state legislatures then will have to decide how high to raise their taxes to fund their programs.

Because a meaningful amount of the federal bureaucracy and mandates will no longer be funded and the state and local government bureaucracy erected to comply with federal dictates would be dismantled, the net impact on Americans of cutting federal taxes and raising states taxes will result in meaningfully lower taxes. This important point bears repeating given our country's fiscal problems. By leveraging competitive federalism, we can meet the needs of Americans more efficiently and more effectively and do so at a lower total cost. With more than forty cents of every federal tax dollar spent on bureaucracy, we can lower the total tax burden on Americans and dedicate a greater level of funding to producing positive outcomes.

By returning programmatic and taxing power over these issues to the states, we will empower state elected officials to experiment and identify solutions that best serve the unique needs of their citizens. The best solutions can serve as models for other states, allowing for differences based on demographic nuances.

Having direct control over the costs of Medicaid, one of the largest components of state budgets, and these other programs will drive greater competition and outcomes. As more citizens look at their paychecks and see the state costs of these programs, they will pay greater attention to how their government is operating and, equally importantly, place greater focus on the quality of individuals being elected to the state legislatures and governors' offices.

ACTION: Ohio's Governor should aggressively lead the fight against the federal government's nationalization of state and local issues.

Key Reform #7: Invest in Ideas and the Infrastructure Needed to Implement Those Ideas

Conservatives have become very good at spouting the rhetoric of the movement, but their actions sometimes fail to back up that rhetoric. You often hear the slogan "ideas have consequences" from conservatives. At the same time, conservatives fail to invest in the production of the ideas needed to reform state and local governments. As a result, we have become pretty good at getting conservatives elected, but then watch as those conservatives go "native" or fail to enact conservative policies.

The amount of conservative money spent across the United States during each election cycle likely exceeds $1 billion, especially if there is a presidential election at stake. Conservatives provide funding to candidates, Republican Party groups, PACs, and (c)(4) advocacy groups. At the same time, the amount of funds donated to conservative national and state think tanks likely totals less than $100 million. The vast majority of that funding goes to national think tanks such as The Heritage Foundation, the American Enterprise Institute, and the Cato Institute. These groups focus almost exclusively on federal policies and issues, thereby leaving mere crumbs at the state and local levels for groups to produce conservative agendas in the fifty states.

And people wonder why electing conservatives does not result in the enactment of conservative policies. Conservative donors must realize that there are two critical halves of the whole that deserve support: the idea generation and infrastructure side (think tanks and supporting infrastructure) and the execution/accountability side (elected officials and (c)(4) groups). Great ideas without elected officials to implement them collect dust on shelves; similarly, elected officials without great ideas get co-opted by the system (inherently more concerned with perpetuating the status quo) and lobbyists (inherently only concerned with their clients' interests).

The State Policy Network is the umbrella organization that helps state-based think tanks in all fifty states. A few state think tanks have robust operations and strong budgets. Most state think tanks make do with few resources. If conservatives want real reform, we must do more to build the idea factories across America.

Here are four qualities that a think tank should possess before you invest in it.

First, it possesses a leader who can articulate a bold policy vision. Leadership really matters because the agenda of the group starts from the top. A milquetoast policy vision just won't cut it given the crises across state and local governments.

Second and equally important is the independence of the group as evidenced by a willingness to criticize "our side." It is easy to criticize liberal-progressive politicians and to praise conservative politicians. It is far harder to criticize conservative politicians, as doing so risks making donors mad and could result in being ostracized by the establishment. Nonetheless, vigorously defending the group's independence is the only way to maintain credibility and to advance a real conservative agenda. After all, if the group is merely a cheerleader for Republicans, then it is subject to the same forces in favor of moderation and status quo as politicians.

Next, it is comprised of a board of directors/trustees of proven non-establishment entrepreneurs and leaders who not only financially contribute substantially to the group, but who also publicly advocate for the group. Board members also must not possess outside conflicts of interest that put the group's independence at risk. The presence of establishment figures will result in a constant state of tension, as those board members will seek to limit or check the intellectual ammunition to satisfy establishment political friends. A similar problem exists if board members have outside financial interests that depend upon access to the establishment or to political leaders. The last thing any think tank leader needs is a board that inhibits action and undermines independence.

Then, the group must publish data-driven reports on the complex issues facing the state. It is easy to produce reports that promote minor changes or nibble on the margins of our problems. Tackling the big issues, however, is far more difficult because those issues tend to be more complex and more vigorously opposed by special interests and left-wing groups. It is also easy to issue reports that fail to include game-changing reforms needed to fix problems. The point of a conservative think tank should be to widen the field of play by producing solutions backed by hard data that drive the debate to the right.

Finally, the group should have a history of widespread financial support from both high and low value donors across the state in which it resides. A group should never be dependent upon only a handful of high donors, as any donor could choose to move its support to another group or hit financial troubles. Similarly, dependence upon one or only a handful of donors will inhibit bold actions for fear of angering those donors and losing support. A broad and diverse base of support indicates to new donors that the group is more than just a one issue or one donor group. Plus, the wider the support across a state, the greater the group's ability to promote its work among the grassroots and pressure politicians to pay attention to the group.

Several existing state-based think tanks meet these four criteria: the Goldwater Institute in Arizona, the Illinois Policy Center in Illinois, and the Oklahoma Council of Public Affairs in Oklahoma. Those groups produce results far in excess of their annual funding.

The think tank is necessary to win the intellectual battle with the left, but it is not sufficient. The think tank must have other infrastructure pieces to successfully win battles and sustain those victories against the perpetual assault from the left.

Because of the failures of JINOs to fairly cover conservative ideas, we must build our own media network in Ohio to produce and to distribute key information to Ohioans. We need investigative reporters who will write the stories the liberal media refuses to write. We also need opposition researchers who will dig up the dirt on those government entities, politicians, and left-wing organizations working to undermine economic freedom and transparency in Ohio. Together, these vital capacities can build a distribution infrastructure that empowers grassroots Ohioans, thereby giving them a chance against the political system and entrenched interests that just want to take more of their hard earned income.

ACTION: Invest in ideas and infrastructure that really do matter.

With the key seven reforms, there is plenty of work to do to fix Ohio and give taxpayers a chance to get ahead. I hope you'll join me in the fight to get these reforms implemented over the expected attempts of the establishment to stop us.

As a sixth generation Ohioan raising the seventh generation, I want an Ohio where our best and brightest stay and make our state great again. With hard work and perseverance, there is no reason why Ohio can't once again be the state of presidents, titans, and ideas.

Today, taxpayers don't stand a chance. We must fix the problems that place taxpayers at such a severe disadvantage. The time for timidity and nibbling on the margins of our problems has long since passed. It is time to act boldly. It is time to act strategically. With a sustained effort and the same level of commitment our Founding Fathers had in starting this great nation, taxpayers can win this critical battle over the future of our state.

ACKNOWLEDGMENT

A special thank you to my patient wife, Jessica, for allowing me the time to write this book.

Next, thank you to Mary McCleary for her assistance in gathering most of the data highlighted in this book. Mary did yeoman's work as a Policy Analyst at the Buckeye Institute to advance sound fiscal policies. There is simply no one better at finding and crunching the data than Mary.

Finally, thank you to Michael Carnuccio, Pam Hall, Bill Jacob, Walt Klein, Chris Littleton, Carl Mayer, and Mary who took the time to review a draft of the manuscript and provided me their honest and very beneficial feedback. The end result is far better because of you.

DISCLOSURE

As a proponent of transparency, I feel it is important to disclose to readers the following items:

- My family owns a home and works in Dublin, Ohio.
- My kids attend Dublin City Schools.
- I serve as an independent contractor writing for The Heritage Foundation and the Oklahoma Council of Public Affairs.
- I am involved as a volunteer in the workplace freedom effort in Ohio.
- My wife works at Cardinal Health.
- My family owns equity interests of less than $10,000 in Chesapeake Energy, Intel, Microsoft, and Peabody Energy.
- I am a member (via my limited teaching over four quarters as an adjunct professor at The Ohio State University) of the State Teachers Retirement System.

SOURCES

For detailed tables containing the data discussed throughout this book, please visit the Opportunity Ohio website at www.opportunityohio.org. The data in this book came from the following sources:

Buckeye Institute for Public Policy Solutions

City of Dublin

Congressional Budget Office

Dublin City Schools

Federation of Tax Administrators

Franklin County Board of Elections

Institute for Justice

National Assessment of Education Progress

Ohio Department of Administrative Services

Ohio Department of Education

Ohio Department of Taxation

Ohio Education Association

Ohio General Assembly

Ohio Office of Budget & Management

Ohio Office of the Governor

Ohio Secretary of State

Organization for Economic Co-Operation and Development

The Tax Foundation

U.S. Bureau of Economic Analysis

U.S. Bureau of Labor Statistics

U.S. Census Bureau

U.S. Department of Labor

U.S. Department of Transportation

ViaMeadia

ABOUT THE AUTHOR

Matt A. Mayer is the President of Provisum Strategies where he provides strategic and tactical political and policy advice to public and private-sector clients. Mayer also serves as President of Opportunity Ohio, as a Visiting Fellow with The Heritage Foundation, America's top think tank, where he writes and speaks on national security and federalism issues, and as a Research Fellow at the Oklahoma Council of Public Affairs. Mayer's first book, *Homeland Security and Federalism: Protecting America from Outside the Beltway (with Foreward by the Honorable Edwin Meese III)*, argued for reversing the federalization of homeland security by returning power to states and localities.

Formerly, Mayer served as the President of the Buckeye Institute for Public Policy Solutions, Ohio's top free market think tank. Under Mayer's leadership, the Buckeye Institute became an influential trendsetter. Mayer also launched an innovative, best-in-class website attracting over 7 million data searches and released several game-changing reports on how best to fix Ohio, including on reducing Ohio's costly governments, reforming criminal justice and Medicaid programs, transforming government pensions for today's economy, and reinvigorating Ohio's systemically weak private sector.

Before joining the Buckeye Institute, Mayer served as a highly rated Adjunct Professor at The Ohio State University where he taught a course comparing responses within the transatlantic alliance to terrorist threats. Mayer was a senior official at the U.S. Department of Homeland Security under the leadership of Secretaries Tom Ridge and Michael Chertoff where he provided DHS leaders with policy and operational advice as the Counselor to the Deputy Secretary and where he headed the $3.5 billion terrorism preparedness office charged with developing initiatives to transform America to meet the demands of a post-9/11 environment.

Mayer came to DHS from Colorado where he served Governor Bill Owens as the Deputy Director for the Department of Regulatory Agencies. Mayer co-developed Colorado's Regulatory Notice system that utilizes electronic mail to notify stakeholders of all proposed regulations before those regulations become final. The Regulatory Notice system earned the Denver Business Journal's 2003 "Innovative Product/Service Award" for making government more transparent and accountable. Prior to joining Governor Owens' team, Mayer served as a deputy in Colorado Senator Wayne Allard's reelection effort in 2002, and ran a widely hailed congressional campaign for a first-time candidate. As a result of his campaign work, the Colorado Statesman selected Mayer for its 2002 "Rising Star Award."

Mayer was a 2007 Lincoln Fellow with The Claremont Institute for the Study of Statesmanship and Political Philosophy and a 2006 American Marshall Memorial Fellow with the German Marshall Fund of the United States. In September 2005, The Ohio State University Alumni Association awarded Mayer the William Thompson Oxley Award for early career achievement. At the age of 29, the Denver Business Journal recognized Mayer as one of Colorado's young leaders by naming him to its "Forty Under 40" list. In 1997, Mayer was the recipient of the ABA-BNA Excellence in Labor & Employment Law Award and was recognized as a Public Service Fellow. He has written articles for law reviews, public policy journals, and newspapers; given testimony to the U.S. Congress, the Texas House and Senate, and the Ohio House and Senate; and appeared on Fox News, C-SPAN, and other major media outlets.

Mayer graduated *cum laude* from the University of Dayton, with a double major in Philosophy and Psychology and received his law degree from The Ohio State University College of Law where he was the Editor in Chief of the Ohio State Journal on Dispute Resolution.

Mayer resides in Dublin, Ohio, with his wife and three children.